ANNE MCALPIN

The Essential Guide To Organized Travel

Pack It Up
The Essential Guide to Organized Travel

Special thanks to the travelers I have met
around the globe who have contributed many
of these invaluable travel tips.

Cover and text design by Roberta Great
Text editing by Whitman & Jo Parker
Illustrations by Holly Herick Design
Cover Photos by David Gibb Photography

ISBN 0-9627263-3-8
Library of Congress Number 90-082758
Printed in the U.S.A.
10 9 8 7 6 5 4 3

Published by Flying Cloud Publishing
For more information, contact:
www.packitup.com

To my father whose sea stories enticed me to travel to the four corners of the world — to experience my own, and my mother, who continually packed my suitcases to ensure that I made it in one piece.

This book is dedicated to my parents, both of whom have made the ultimate journey.

Table of Contents

"If you want to get away from it all,
don't take it all with you."

Anne McAlpin

- 1 -
Before You Go

"If you want to get away from it all, don't take it all with you." This always gets a big laugh at my **Pack It Up** seminars. Most people know they pack too much when they travel, but aren't really sure how to bring less. How do you travel safely, pack everything you need and travel lightly? After reading this book, you'll be on your way.

This book is a compilation of over 25 years of travel tips that I've discovered on the road. Some I've learned the hard way, many I've learned from more experienced travelers I've met along the way. There are even a few tips that I learned while studying in Europe and realized too late that I didn't have the budget or the strength to carry everything I thought I needed!

You'll find valuable plane tips I've picked up from other frequent flyers (whom I'm always interviewing in the air) and cruise tips learned while working aboard cruise ships. Check out the Family Travel chapter for invaluable tips on traveling with children and find out how to save money on laundry services in Laundry on the Go.

One of the biggest concerns of women traveling alone is security. I've addressed this important topic in the security chapter, which also includes tips on how to prepare your home before you leave, and what to pack in your security wallet.

You'll find invaluable luggage tips, packing tips and

yes, even tips on how to get through airport security more efficiently using plastic bags.

Note my all-time favorite tips highlighted in special **"AM FAVE"** boxes throughout the book.

For your convenience, there is the Ultimate Traveler's Checklist at the end of this book (and available at **www.packitup.com**).

This book is full of secret travel tips I've discovered from traveling to over 67 countries that will make any trip safer and a whole lot more fun. And remember that "travel" happens the minute you step outside your front door. Whether you're flying to Europe, taking a cruise of a lifetime or driving to a family reunion, you still have to pack to get there. So, let's get started.

Three important steps to a successful trip:

Read, Ask and Plan

Read anything you can get your hands on about your destination.

Check out the travel section in the Sunday newspaper, the internet and travel guidebooks. Before you rush out and spend money on unnecessary travel books, visit the library to narrow your search. Researching your destination online is another good option. If you don't have access to a computer, most libraries provide them, which will open up access to a wealth of information to any destination in the world.

Ask family, friends and travel agents questions about your destination. People love to share their experiences and their knowledge. How often have we all received invaluable information through a casual conversation?

Your reading should prompt many questions and now is the time to find the answers.

Plan ahead. Advanced planning can save you money and help alleviate stress further down the road. By planning and asking, you may receive many discounts that you didn't know existed, from pre-booking savings to off-season and senior discounts.

Tips

- There's nothing more valuable than a good travel agent. Many people do not realize the amount of time and money travel agencies can save them. Keep in mind, there is usually a fee involved. However, time is money, and for many this fee is worth the time they would spend searching and planning on their own. Call and compare prices for all your travel needs.

- Surf the internet. Many great travel bargains have been found on the internet. However, be sure you understand any restrictions that might apply to any purchases. And, as mentioned above, there's nothing like working with a reputable travel agent to protect you and your travel plans. The majority of travelers still prefer to use the internet for research rather than making purchases.

- Read your travel documents upon receipt. It's all too common for travelers to be left stranded because they didn't double check the departure date or time on their ticket.

- Just like brands of food, different travel agencies have different features and benefits. Ask friends for recommendations.

3

- If you prefer the phone to the internet, you can call the airlines listed in the phone book to find out about any special deals.

- Always reconfirm your domestic airline ticket 24 hours in advance and your international ticket 72 hours in advance.

- Most airlines provide online check-in and pre-printed boarding passes you can access before you head to the airport. This saves valuable time.

- Obtain or renew your passport for International travel. The normal processing time to obtain a passport is six weeks, but it can take longer during peak travel months. Locate the passport facility nearest you at the State Department's website **www.state.gov**.

- For an additional fee you can expedite processing your passport (usually a worthwhile expense).

- If your travels require visas (another good reason for using a travel agent) you should apply for your passport at least six months in advance to allow time to acquire them.

- Have a full medical and dental check-up prior to traveling.

- Obtain or renew your International Driving Permit if necessary.

- Review your travel, homeowners, automobile, and medical insurance policies to determine coverage for trip cancellation, interruption, loss, theft, accident, or injury while traveling overseas. If necessary, consider additional coverage.

- Research whether special precautions (such as inoculations, malaria pills, etc.) are required for travel to your destination.

- Check with your pet sitters, plant sitters and child care provider. Have a second choice on standby just in case someone has to cancel at the last minute.

- Obtaining a calling card from your long distance telephone company before leaving home (or buying a pre-paid phone card) will expedite any calls you must make and puts an end to searching for correct coins in foreign currency.

- Contact your cell phone provider to find out if you can use your cell phone while traveling. There are also International Cell Phones available.

- Be sure your bills are paid and up to date if you plan to be gone for an extended period of time. Better yet, pre-pay them and you won't come home to a stack of overdue bills. Most banks offer automated bill-pay online.

- Photocopy the pages in your travel guide for your own use so you don't have to take the entire book along. Or simply tear out the applicable chapters.

- Check the expiration dates on your credit cards, passport, driver's license, medical certificates, camera film, vitamins, medications, etc.

- Notify your credit card companies that you'll be traveling and using your cards at your destination. Also reconfirm credit limits.

- Put your name and business address in your coat. They are always being left in restaurants, planes and trains.

- Make a note, as a reminder, of any special events such as birthdays and anniversaries that will occur while you're away.

- Bring along note cards for celebrations on your trip. This saves last minute shopping (and money). Of course, you might like the charm of greetings cards in another language.

- Pack cards with pictures from your home region to share with others you meet along the way.

- Purchase some sticky address labels and spend an evening addressing them to all your family and friends (or print the addresses from your printer). Then while traveling, there's no need to haul your address book with you. Just peel and stick. It's easier and faster and you will know who did and didn't receive postcards!

- Bring self-address labels for your own use — for safety, you may want to use a PO Box. Using them as return address labels, for filling out forms in stores or checking into hotels, makes life easier when you are busy and/or tired.

Research Your Destination

- Check the video store for videos about your destination or ask your travel agent. They don't have to be travel guides specifically. For example, you may see feature or fictional films about France that include local customs, history, and scenery.

- Look into educational tours related to your profession. They could be tax-deductible and save you money.

- Call, write or e-mail the Chamber of Commerce or National Tourist Office for additional information on your destination. Ask specifically for maps, dates of events, or about anything you are interested in.

- Research tour companies. Specialized tours, such as sports tours, art tours and wine tours are a great way to meet people with the same interests and will often save you money.

- Minimize culture shock by learning about the lifestyle and foods of your destination ahead of time.

- Familiarize yourself with local customs and political differences to avoid offensive behavior, inappropriate dress and breaking any laws.

- It's always helpful and fun to learn a few words and key phrases in a foreign language. Borrow some language tapes from your local library or download to your iPod® to take with you. If you're really serious about learning a foreign language, check college extension courses.

*"I haven't been everywhere,
but it's on my list."*

Susan Sontag

- 2 -
Security at Home and En-Route

The most important safety tip I can offer is **to be aware of your surroundings**. In this day and age, any city can be dangerous, even your own home town, no matter what size or population. The idea is not to travel in fear but to pay attention to some important details.

The following tips will help you protect yourself, your home and your property.

Many of these suggestions apply to everyday circumstances, and most of them are common sense.

General Home Security

Before you leave:

❏ Lock all your valuables in a safe deposit box.

❏ Put timers on several lights in your house. For a good deterrent, leave your radio tuned to a talk show.

❏ Obtain an engraving pen from your local library or police station and mark your valuable electronic equipment with an I.D. number. Secure the list in your safe-deposit box.

❏ In cold climate zones, turn off your hot water heater and defrost the refrigerator in case of a power failure. If you live in temperate climates, turn down your furnace and air conditioning.

Unplug your appliances, such as your computer, stereo and television in case of power surges.

❏ Affix screws into window frames to secure them from outside opening. Ask at your hardware store for additional ideas.

❏ For added security to sliding glass doors, place a broom handle in the track. Also, a board across the center of the window placed on two rivets will do the same trick.

Although weekend outings may require no arrangements for your home, longer trips require some consideration. Don't advertise that you're away by having your newspapers pile up in your driveway or by allowing your lawn to grow wild.

❏ Have your mail held at the post office until your return.

❏ Have your newspaper stopped or have a reliable neighbor pick it up everyday.

❏ Don't forget to stop UPS delivery or other delivery services that may frequent your home.

❏ Hire a gardener to take care of your garden and keep your lawn mowed.

❏ If you don't have an answering machine, put your telephone on the lowest ring setting so that no one outside can hear the continual ringing.

To help give the appearance that you are home, the following are other things you can ask a neighbor or relative to do while you are away.

❏ Place their garbage in your cans once in awhile.

❏ Shovel snow from your sidewalk and/or driveway.

❏ Park their car in your driveway after 5 pm and on the weekends once in awhile.

❏ Check your mailbox periodically for mail or advertising that might have slipped through.

❏ Check your front porch and door for advertising flyers.

❏ Keep a set of your car keys in case there is a fire in your garage, or any other reason your cars need to be moved.

❏ Check the inside of your home periodically in case there has been any kind of water damage, frozen pipes, electrical outage, or anything that they might be able to assist with until you return home.

❏ If you have an answering machine, ask a friend to check it and answer any messages that sound important. Calls unreturned for any length of time are a good give-away that you are not at home.

❏ Leave contact information and insurance numbers with a neighbor just in case.

❏ Keep a list of all these security tips and check them off as you complete them. Take a copy with you for ease of mind.

Security En Route

● Always, be sure to travel with a security wallet. See page 27 for more information.

● A card with telephone numbers and names of relatives can be very helpful in case of emergency. Don't forget to include a neighbor in case you can't remember if you turned off the iron. Keep one copy with you and e-mail a copy to yourself for safe keeping and global online access in case you lose the list.

- In a place other than your wallet, carry a list of the items in your wallet, including the phone numbers to report the items lost or stolen.

- If traveling with your cell phone, pre-program important numbers into it, including an ICE # "In Case of Emergency."

- When traveling alone, always use valet parking when available. Walking through a deserted parking lot alone is not a good idea anywhere. Be sure to give your car only to a uniformed valet.

- NEVER carry anything for anyone for any reason.

- Keep your distance from stray luggage and packages left unattended in airports and other public places.

- Never leave your luggage unattended.

Hotel Tips

- Always guarantee your hotel room reservation with a major credit card, just in case you're delayed. When traveling alone, always be sure to have reservations.

- When checking into a hotel, never give your home address for security reasons. Instead, give your work address (or PO Box).

- Most hotels no longer print room numbers on keys. In the event they do, be sure to keep your key out of site. This could lead to unwelcome strangers seeing your room number.

- If available, request a room near the elevator, to avoid the chance of someone following you and walking long distances in empty hallways.

- Verify the exit route from your room upon arrival at your hotel.

- Don't leave a "Please Make Up My Room" sign on the door, which advertises an empty room.

- Avoid staying in a room in remote parts of the hotel or next to exit stairways.

- In a hotel room or aboard ship, memorize the location of the nearest emergency exit. Count the number of doors in case of heavy smoke. Also, this works on planes. In case the lights go out, you should count the number of rows to the nearest exit as you board the plane.

- When traveling with children, be sure they know the name and address of the hotel. Put a business card of the hotel in their pocket.

- Don't leave any valuables in your room when you leave. Experienced thieves know how to find what they're looking for.

- Place valuables in the hotel safe.

- Ask the front desk which streets and neighborhoods to avoid.

- To prevent extra hotel telephone charges and taxes, use a telephone calling card or cell phone.

Take some small 'post-it' notes to use on your hotel mirror as reminders. "Remember your travel alarm," "passport in the hotel safe," and so on.

Hotel Comfort Items

Whether you're on the road for two days or two weeks, it's nice to have some comfort items with you. Here are some "comforting" ideas:

Battery Operated Travel Alarm Clock

Don't rely on a hotel wake up call when you have to be at the train station at 6 am. Have a back-up plan even if your hotel room provides an alarm clock! You might not set it correctly. Bring extra batteries. Put fresh batteries in your clock before the trip. Most cell phones also have an alarm feature on them.

Night Light

Take a night light for unfamiliar hotel rooms or ship cabins. It lights the bathroom in the middle of the night. Leave a note in your bag to remind yourself to pack it when you leave the hotel. Bring a converter if necessary.

Queen/King Size Top Bed Sheet

Ever wonder when the last time the bed spread was washed in your hotel room? Here's my secret: Upon check-in, I request an extra sheet. Then I take off the bedspread and put the sheet on top of the blanket to protect me from a scratchy (and maybe not-so-clean) blanket. Leave a note on the bed in the morning to please leave the bed as is so housekeeping won't put the bedspread back on top of your clean sheet. Or you can travel with a lightweight silk sheet. This way you know it's clean and it provides a bit of luxury away from home.

Fitted Bed Sheet

Don't you just hate it when you go to a hotel and sleep on the bed and the bottom sheet moves all over the bed? Consider taking your own fitted bottom bed sheet (shrinks down to almost nothing in a compression bag).

Collapsible Water Bottle

Save space and travel with a water bottle that folds up when empty. Here's a tip: I can't get to sleep with cold feet so I take two: One for drinking water and one I fill up with hot tap water as a foot warmer.

Travel Toilet Paper

On my travels in Europe, I often stay at "European-style" small hotels — clean, comfortable, but not always stocked with items I like, such as soft toilet paper. A small roll of toilet paper can be flattened, taking up very little space and adding little weight to your bag.

Washcloths

Don't forget a wash cloth, an item sometimes not found in smaller hotels. Baby washcloths are small and quick drying.

More Hotel Tips

- Always have a stash of one dollar bills for vending machines and for tipping the maid.

- Remember that if you did forget something, most hotels have items available at the front desk (either complimentary or for sale).

- Most US hotels have hair dryers in the room. International hotels, however, seldom provide hair dryers so call ahead to confirm. You might be able to borrow one from the front desk.

- If you are particular about your pillowcase, take your own. A brightly colored pillowcase will be less likely left behind. They also come in handy for dirty clothes when packing for the trip home.

- Hairspray makes for a quick room freshener in a pinch.

- Ever wonder what to do with the complimentary shower caps in your hotel room? In hotels where your room is miles away from the ice machine, toss a couple shower caps in your bag when you leave for the day, then on your way back to the room, use them as an 'ice bucket' of sorts.

- Another use for a hotel shower cap is to bring it home and use it in the kitchen to cover large, odd shaped bowls.

- Sometimes the water at a hotel is heavily chlorinated. Using melted ice from the ice machine often creates a more pleasing drink of water.

- Concierges at major hotels are an invaluable source of information.

- Packing cubes are perfect for hotels. Nobody wants to put their personal items (like clean underwear) in a drawer when you don't know what was in it before you checked in. A cube will also keep everything together (like a drawer within a drawer) so nothing slides to the back and gets left behind. See page 28.

- Create a mini-spa in your hotel room. Collect travel sizes and samples of bath gel, hair products, foot scrubs, etc. They're especially great after a long day of sightseeing.

Life is either a daring adventure or nothing.

Helen Keller

- 3 -
Tips for Women Traveling Solo

There is an old proverb that says, "It is better to travel alone than with a bad companion." I've traveled alone and with a bad companion and whole heartedly agree: solo is much better! For years, women have asked me, "Aren't you scared to travel alone?" I'm happy to say that I've never encountered a really dangerous situation, because I try very hard not to put myself into one. Admittedly, there have been times when I've felt uncomfortable, like an unfortunate incident in a movie theater in Spain! Remember, however, things can happen just as easily at home as they can on the road.

I've traveled on my own for over 27 years and have only been robbed once. Guess where? Yes, in my own country in broad daylight. When I travel, I am always aware of my surroundings. However, when I was in a rush while shopping in downtown USA, I wasn't paying attention and my wallet was stolen right out of my unzipped purse. Silly me!

In addition to the aforementioned security tips, here are some more tips for women traveling solo.

- In the unlikely event a desk clerk announces your room number loudly, ask for a different one. Strangers may be within hearing and harass you later. Fortunately, hotels are aware of this and henceforth are very cautious.

- Always use the "peep-hole" in your door to see who is there before opening it. If you are the least bit uncomfortable, call the front desk immediately.

- When traveling alone, treat yourself to a bouquet of flowers to brighten up your hotel room. Use the ice bucket for a vase.

- Always leave the light on in your hotel room and the "Do Not Disturb" sign on the door (after the maid has cleaned) when you leave, to eliminate any unwanted visitors. And leave your TV turned on. While you are inside your hotel room, always keep the door locked (if it isn't automatically) and the chain across the lock (if provided).

- To make you feel more at ease when dining alone, take a book or magazine to the table. Keep in mind that paperback books are hard to read if your meal requires two hands to eat.

- For safety, it's a good idea to travel with a whistle, which can be used to alert those around you that you need assistance.

- If you are a single woman traveler and find yourself in the situation of a foreign man harassing you, sit beside a local woman on the train or bus, or walk directly behind women. Even though there's often a language barrier, women tend to stick together and can understand your look of distress towards an overly-friendly male pursuer.

- Sit in the front of the bus, train or restaurant you are in. Take precautions that you may not necessarily take at home: Don't walk through parks alone if you feel the least bit nervous. Don't walk outside in the evening without a companion. Don't unwillingly put yourself in a position in which you might be endangered.

- Always travel with a flashlight so you won't be caught in the dark. I prefer a small travel size flashlight that clips onto my day bag so I'm never without one.

- Carry 2 plastic coated S-hooks (found in hardware stores) in your purse or carry-on. Use them in the hinge area in the bathroom stalls to hold your tote/ purse/coat to keep them off the floor when there are no hooks available.

- In addition to security wallets, specialty travel clothing that feature zippered "secret" pockets also help you avoid being the victim of a pick pocket.

"People don't take trips – trips take people."

John Steinbeck

- 4 -

Packing Smart for Airport Security

We travel differently these days. In the past, my philosophy was always to try to carry all my luggage on the plane. However, with all the time needed for security screening, and newer, larger airports, it's a lot easier (in most cases) to check your big bag and carry-on only what you need for the first 2 days of your trip.

If you are an experienced or business traveler and have packing down to a science, continue to carry-on everything you need. Early boarding and priority seating are just a few of the benefits of being a frequent traveler. Just having the first crack at the overhead compartments feels like a benefit these days.

However, if you're like most travelers, you're not flying first class and you don't usually gaze into an empty overhead bin. And most of us don't have the height and upper body strength to balance a 25 pound bag over our heads and stuff it into an already overcrowded overhead compartment.

So, in summary, if you can't handle your own bag on the plane, check it. Wouldn't it be great if everyone was able to stow their bags and take their seats in a timely manner?

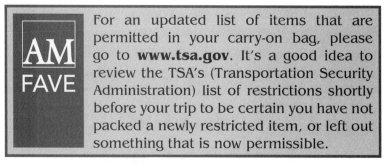

For an updated list of items that are permitted in your carry-on bag, please go to **www.tsa.gov**. It's a good idea to review the TSA's (Transportation Security Administration) list of restrictions shortly before your trip to be certain you have not packed a newly restricted item, or left out something that is now permissible.

Travelers are currently limited to the amount of liquids they can pack in their carry-on bag.

Currently permitted per person is 1 quart-sized, clear, plastic, zip-top bag containing:

- 3 ounce bottles (or less) of liquids in your carry-on bag. However, this might have changed by the time you read this. If in doubt, put your liquids in your checked bag. Again, since allowable carry-on rules are changing, go to www.tsa.gov.

- Prescription medications, baby formula and milk (when traveling with an infant or toddler) are allowed in quantities exceeding three ounces and are not required to be in the Ziploc® bag. Declare these items for inspection at the checkpoint. Again, I recommend you check www.tsa.gov for an up-to-the-minute list of restricted items before each trip.

Tips

- If you're planning to check luggage, you should arrive at the airport up to 2 hours prior to your flight departure time to allow for security processing and baggage screenings. For International flights, check with your specific carrier.

- Travel with two forms of photo ID. If you misplace one, you're covered.

- Bring a boarding pass, ticket, or ticket confirmation, such as a printed itinerary, as well as a government-issued photo ID.

- If you have a medical implant (or other device), it's recommended that you advise the security officer. Bring evidence verifying your medical condition if it is likely to set off the alarm on the metal detector. Keep this information with your travel documents.

- Choose bags with a single packing space over those with multiple pockets or inside pouches. It makes the process of screening bags through X-ray or hand checks easier.

- Place everything possible inside resealable plastic bags.

I always pack my underwear and personal items in plastic bags. I'm happier knowing that Security personnel is not touching my undies. I think they're happier, too!

- To prevent delays at the security checkpoint, think about what you're wearing before you leave for the airport. Some larger accessory pieces like belt buckles and shoes or boots with metal shanks will set off alarms and cause you to be searched. Delays may cause you to miss your flight.

- Be prepared to demonstrate that your electronic gear works, including laptops, cameras and cell phones.

- If traveling with a laptop, be sure it's in a padded case for protection. Never pack your laptop in your checked bag. For a list of security-friendly computer bags go to **www.packitup.com**.

- Upon arrival, be sure to go directly to the baggage claim area to claim your luggage. Unfortunately, most airports no longer have security agents checking bag claim tickets. Be sure you're the only one walking away with your bags.

- Above all, if you are searched, keep your cool and be pleasant.

Some great travel essentials to help you "fly" through airport security:

Luggage Locks

It's ok to lock your bags, if you use a TSA (Transportation Security Administration) accepted lock.

The TSA allows you to secure your bag with these approved locks. If airport security needs to inspect your checked bag and you're not with it, they use their pass key to open it. These new locks allow TSA to open your locks and re-lock your bags, sending them quickly on their way. For more information on these locks, please go to **www.packitup.com**.

Remember: Never pack anything valuable in your checked bag. Always keep valuables with you in your carry-on bag.

Luggage ID

All bags are required to have an ID tag. Be sure to fill out the tags at home so you don't have to do it while standing in line at check-in. To help make sure you know which bags are yours while going through security, bright neon luggage tags are the answer! Never put your home address on your luggage ID tag. Please see page 43.

Boarding Pass Holder

This travel essential hangs around your neck like a security badge. It's made specifically to organize your travel documents for use while in the airport. Individual pockets for your boarding pass, photo ID and passport make it a breeze to show your documents numerous times while juggling your carry-on bags on each leg of your trip. Once at your destination, pack it away until your return trip home. (Tip: for easy access, slip a few dollars in for coffee/newspaper/tips).

Security Wallet

The previously mentioned boarding pass holder is for ease at the airport only. A security wallet is a must for all types of travel. You wear a security wallet under your clothing so your valuables are hidden and not easily accessible. Wearing your valuables inside your clothing (except for photo ID), is not only smart but is one less thing security has to check. Be certain, however, not to carry anything metal inside so you won't have to take it off at security checkpoints. Upon arrival, transfer the items from your boarding pass holder to your security wallet for added security and safety.

There are many types of security wallets. My favorite is the silk waist wallet: It's large enough to accommodate my passport and important travel documents. See the security wallet checklist on page 32.

Packing Folders and Cubes

Folders and cubes make getting through security easier. Folders organize your items like shirts and pants, allowing you to neatly fold and stack your clothing, while providing security easy access.

The best way to organize small clothing items (like socks and undies), is packing cubes. They are made with see-through mesh netting or plastic, making it easy for security (and you) to see what's inside each cube. (Plastic zip-top bags are another option).

Compression Bags

Simply put, these are the best kept secret travelers need to know about. You'll make Security's job easier since they can view what's packed inside each clear plastic bag.

And, compression bags can create 3 times more space in your carry-on bag. For more info on these bags, please go to page 70.

Wheeled Tote Bags, Organizers and Computer Bags

Whether you're traveling on vacation or business, a wheeled carry-on is the perfect solution for large airports. As mentioned, organize your items in compression bags and folders and then place inside your bag to expedite your trip through security. If traveling with a computer, be sure it's protected inside a padded case. Also, have it easily accessible for inspection. Always tape your business card on your computer in case you're separated. (Tip: Toss in a collapsible tote bag for extra purchases along the way.)

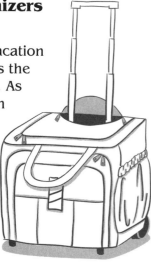

Insiders Tip

In case you have to take your shoes off to go through the security checkpoint, wear shoes that are easy to slip on and off.

29

*"If you look like your passport photo,
you're too ill to travel."*

Will Kommen

- 5 -

Money, Passports and Other Travel Documents

The most important tip regarding money and documents for a trip is: start early. Too often, we hear nightmare accounts of friends forgetting to apply well in advance for their passport or visa and they wind-up anxiously awaiting the arrival of the document, hoping their trip will not be in jeopardy.

Depending on your destination, you may need a passport, a visa, or only a driver's license and birth certificate. If you are traveling as part of a tour-group or cruise, visa services may be included as part of your package. Be certain to discuss this with your travel agent as soon as you begin planning your trip. If you will be responsible for your own documents, it may be worth the extra expense to use a professional passport and visa service to complete the process for you. The last thing you want is to be detained in an airport — where nobody speaks English — because your visa application wasn't processed properly! Please see the resources page at the back of this book for a list of websites containing information on how to obtain passports and visa applications.

Once you have your passport, visas, and inoculations, the following suggestions will help you avoid misfortunes on your journey.

Security Wallet

The most important item you'll pack for any trip is your security wallet. I use mine not only when I travel internationally, but also in large cities and public events. There are many styles of security wallets, the two most common are worn around the neck and worn around the waist. As mentioned earlier, I prefer the type that goes around my waist. I prefer the double zipper wallet for better organization. Most men prefer a neck wallet.

The secret to being comfortable while wearing a waist security wallet is be sure it's silk with an elastic waistband. If you tuck in your shirt, wear it over your shirt, but below the waistband of your pants. Be certain it is never visible. If you don't tuck your shirt in, the silk is really important, as it's more comfortable against your skin than synthetic fabrics.

Security Wallet Checklist:

- ❏ Passport
- ❏ 2 major credit cards
- ❏ ATM Card
- ❏ Drivers License/Photo ID
- ❏ Large amounts of cash
- ❏ Airline/Rail/Bus tickets
- ❏ Copy of itinerary
- ❏ Recent pictures of people you're traveling with, especially children
- ❏ Immunization records
- ❏ Phone Card

I'm always asked what type of money I prefer to travel with and here's my answer: Everything. I carry 2 major credit cards, US cash, cash in the currency of the country I'm traveling and an ATM card. Travelers checks are not widely accepted anymore. Check with your travel agent before buying travelers checks.

I travel with 2 major credit cards because I have been in many situations where a hotel or restaurant will not accept one card, but will the other. I also pack a photo copy of the front and back of my credit cards just in-case I need to call and cancel them. Note the back of the card includes the cancellation numbers.

The Ultimate Travelers Handbag

For most trips, I travel with one handbag which easily transitions from day to evening: A 2-in-1 shoulder bag/ backpack. Wear it over your shoulder across the front of your body for security in the city (women who wear their purse hanging behind them can invite problems) then convert it into a backpack when you're away from crowds. Black is a good color choice as you can then wear it to dinner in the evening.

Here's the secret: I keep enough cash for the day in this bag for lunch, small souvenirs, museum tickets, etc. (approx. $75 cash). This way, I only need to access my security wallet for a major purchase. I only do this when in a secure location, i.e. at a bank or inside my hotel room.

If by chance my 2-in-1 bag is lost or stolen, I'm only out my camera, some money, souvenirs, etc. My passport and valuables are still safely tucked-away in my security wallet. Keeping your passport and important documents in a security wallet is a much safer way to travel.

For more information, go to **www.packitup.com**.

Tips

- Always photocopy your passport and credit cards before leaving home. Take the copy with you and keep in a safe place separate from the originals. If you need those numbers, use the photocopies to help you report lost or stolen documents. Also, leave a copy at home in case of emergency.

- In addition to a photocopy of your passport, also scan your passport ID page into a computer file and e-mail it to yourself at a secure web-based e-mail address (hotmail, yahoo, etc.) If you have access to the internet and a printer, you will always have access to a copy of your passport.

- Always keep airline, travel and personal phone numbers easily accessible in your wallet. If your flight has been canceled or delayed, move them to an outer pocket of your carry-on.

- Carry extra passport photos in case you need to replace your passport or need additional visas.

- Glue a small piece of Ultra Suede to the back side of your passport so it won't slip out of your passport carrier easily.

- Place a small identifying sticker on the upper right-hand corner of your passport (outside) so it's easy to distinguish when traveling with a group.

- When traveling in really questionable areas, for extra security, wear two concealed security wallets, one around your neck and one around your waist. In case someone demands your money, give them the "fake" wallet which only has a little bit of money in it.

Tips for Traveling with Cash

- In case the banks are closed upon arrival, take a small amount of cash ($75) in local currency for use for porters, taxis or buses.

- Prior to leaving, research the current exchange rates of the countries you're traveling to. Write them down and keep them in your wallet for quick reference.

- Don't forget to take a small amount of your own country's currency to use upon departure from and arrival to your home city.

- Carry small amounts of cash (.50 cents to $1.00) for bathroom attendants — a custom of many countries and often required to receive toilet paper!

- Don't flash large amounts of cash in the open.

- Never carry your wallet in your back pocket.

Tips for Credit Cards

- Call your credit card company and let them know the countries you're traveling to and check your credit limits.

- Travel only with the major credit cards you plan to use or will need in case of an emergency. Leave all others at home.

- When traveling with a companion, make sure that each of you takes different credit cards if they are in the same name. Therefore, if one is lost and you have to cancel it, you have a back-up card. Also, you will have a higher total credit limit on two cards just in case you decide to extend your holiday or need more funds.

35

- It's a good idea to carry one credit card separately from the rest. If the others are lost or stolen you'll still have one major credit card.

- Consider purchasing your airline ticket with a major credit card in case the airline goes under and you lose your money. A credit card company usually has larger resources for such situations.

- Ask which credit cards are accepted before dining or purchasing something. This saves embarrassing situations.

- If you are a serious shopper and think you'll spend everything at the start of your trip, consider sending money to designated destinations on your itinerary.

- If you're traveling in a country which still makes carbon copies of your credit card purchases, be sure to tear up them up. This helps assure that no one can find your credit card number and misuse it.

ATM's

- Don't forget to take your ATM card as an alternative to credit cards.

- Find-out in advance from your bank your numerical/alphabetical PIN numbers, as it differs from country to country and the availability of ATM's.

- For security sake, never use an ATM if you don't feel comfortable with strangers standing near you.

- Whenever possible, use an ATM inside a bank for safety.

- It's always good idea to use an ATM on workday mornings. In case there is a problem there is more time to have it solved before the close of business.

- Check the "fee per-transaction" before you leave on a trip, as these fees can add up quickly.

Customs

- Keep a list of all your purchase receipts for your return home through customs. For ease, record them in your travel journal at the end of each day. This allows you to keep track of your travels and expenditures at the same time.

- While some people consider it a challenge to bring undeclared items through customs, this can be a disastrous and expensive ending to a nice trip.

- Pack all your purchases in the same piece of carry-on luggage in case customs asks to see them. This is safer and saves time while clearing customs.

Tips on Tipping

Many people don't know the origin of the word tips: To Insure Prompt Service

Since tipping can be a very personal matter, the following guide is just that - a guide.

Your tip should reflect the service you receive whether exceptional or poor.

Be sure to always read the bill carefully. In many parts of the world, a gratuity has automatically been added. Keep some small bills in an outside pocket so you don't have to open your wallet at an inconvenient time. If you're giving someone a particularly nice tip, be sure to hand it to them directly. Please see page 119 for cruise ship tipping.

TIPPING GUIDE	
Bellman	$1 - $2 per bag
Doorman	$1 - $2 per bag
Hotel Maid	$1 per day
Room Service	Usually included in bill
Food Servers	15% - 20%
Bartender	15% - 20%
Concierge	$5 - $10
Coat Check	$1
Curbside Sky Cap	$2 per bag
Taxi Drivers	15% - 20%
Bus Tour Driver	$1 - $2 day
Bus Tour Guide	$2 - $5 day

- 6 -
Luggage Tips

My most important luggage tip: Ensure that your luggage is in working order before your trip. Second to you, your luggage is the most important thing to survive your trip. Most travelers find out the hard way that the first three letters in the word "luggage" spell "lug."

Examine the hinges, wheels, seams, straps, zippers, and handles for wear and tear. Most large luggage stores and shoe repair shops can make any necessary repairs.

If you are in the market for new luggage, take into consideration your type of travel. Ask friends and family what their favorite piece of luggage is and why. And before you purchase your luggage, be sure to lift and carry it or roll it around the store once or twice to see if it's manageable. (If possible, see how it rolls on an escalator for ease in airports and hotels).

Do not buy cheap luggage. The mental anguish is not worth the savings. Warning: designer luggage will be stolen before old, worn luggage every time, so consider your luggage purchases seriously. A middle-of-the-road purchase is usually the safest bet.

If you have luggage that is still usable but you'd like to upgrade to a newer bag with better features, here's a suggestion: Donate your used luggage to your favorite charity and treat yourself to a new bag.

When purchasing new luggage, look for good wheels,

expandable luggage and luggage with self-repairing zippers.

Carry-on and Checked Baggage Guidelines

The most important tip is to call your airline or check online to find out the current baggage allowances for your trip. Guidelines change. The last thing you want is to spend valuable vacation dollars on over-sized or overweight bags.

The following is a guideline of what is allowed on most airlines:

Carry-on Bags

Most airlines allow one carry-on bag and one personal item such as a purse, briefcase, or laptop computer on the plane. A carry-on bag must fit under your seat or in the overhead bin. Its dimensions should not be more than 9 x 14 x 22 (length + height + width) or 45 linear inches (the length, height and width added together).

Since there are exceptions, check with your airline.

Airlines may require your bag be checked if it cannot be safely stowed on a particular flight. Be prepared and know what items you'll need for your journey in case this happens (i.e. medication, valuables, etc).

In case your carry-on is not allowed on the plane at the last minute, plan ahead. Pack important items (like medicine, jewelry, glasses, etc.) in a plastic bag for quick and easy retrieval. A quick "grab and go" bag is the best way to go!

The maximum weight allowance for most airlines' carry-on bag is 40 pounds, but a maximum weight of 15 pounds for ease in handling is suggested. Again, check with your specific carrier for their allowances which vary depending on plane structure.

Most airlines exempt the following personal items from the one piece limit:

- Child safety seats and strollers for ticketed children

- Assistive devices (i.e. canes, crutches, etc)

- Outer garments (i.e. coats, hats, etc.)

Checked Bags

For domestic travel, you may generally check up to two bags, but additional fees may be incurred. Check with your airline.

The two checked bags may be up to 62 inches (length + width + height) and 50 pounds each. Generally, you may substitute bowling, fishing, golfing, or skiing equipment for one piece of the two allowable checked pieces. Confirm in advance.

Oversized and Overweight Bags

If your bag is heavier or larger than the linear inches permitted by the airline (add up the total of the width, length and height) you will be charged an additional fee. Get out your measuring tape in advance and step on your bathroom scale with your bag to verify you're within guidelines. An easier method to weigh bags is to use a digital luggage scale. Chronic over-packers should weigh their bag before they start on their trip, and pack a scale (as it's under 10 oz.). Then weigh your bag coming home.

Excess Baggage

With long check-in lines and ever-increasing airline baggage restrictions, some travelers are sending their bags ahead via luggage-shipping services. These services will pick up your luggage at your home, office or hotel, and deliver it to your destination overnight. An alternative (and less expensive means) is to ship your bag via UPS Ground or the Postal Service. Compare rates and transit times to see what works best for you.

Delayed and Damaged Luggage

Unfortunately, it happens. If your bags don't come off the conveyor belt or are damaged, a report should be filed at the Baggage Service Office immediately before leaving the airport.

My Favorite Bags

For light trips, with no checked luggage, my favorite bags are:

1) 22" wheeled suitcase

2) Zippered tote bag

3) Convertible day into evening handbag

For longer trips and checked luggage:

1) 24" wheeled suitcase

2) 16" rolling tote bag

3) Zippered tote bag

4) Convertible day into evening handbag

Depending on the trip, I usually check my large bag (24") and carry-on the other bags.

The secret to being able to carry-on three bags is: I pack my purse/day bag inside the collapsible tote which results in having just two bags: one carry-on and one personal.

The reason I have two wheeled bags is that once I check my large bag, I'm stuck without wheels. Most airports are huge, and this way I have a wheeled tote bag which allows me to breeze along the terminals without carrying all that weight on my shoulders.

Upon arrival, or at baggage claim, I simply attach the 16" rolling tote to the 22" or 24" wheeled suitcase and place the tote bag (with my day bag inside) on top. This way I'm only rolling one bag behind me and there's no need to search for porters or carts.

Luggage ID Tips

- Never put your home address on your luggage ID tag. A sure sign that you are not at home is when you arrive at your destination and your bag is circling the baggage terminal in another airport forever. It is not mandatory in all airports to show your baggage claim check upon entering or exiting the baggage terminal, and anyone may have access to your luggage and home address on the tag.

- Put your travel agent, a relative, a trusted neighbor, or your office/work number contact information on your ID tag. Of course, leave a detailed copy of your itinerary, including hotel addresses, with someone you trust. It does no good for airport personnel to call your home, as there wouldn't be anyone there to answer!

- Place a copy of your ID tag and itinerary inside your luggage in case you are separated from it. This way, it stands a chance of catching-up with you. Also, tags can get torn off along the way due to frequent handling.

- Always place an ID tag on your carry-on bag as well.

- Tie bright ribbons on each piece of luggage (whether checked or carry-on) as well for easy ID and inclusion with a lost luggage report. Do not use red ribbon. The majority of black luggage has red ribbons. Try another color!

- Before leaving home: take a photo of your luggage (including carry-ons). Use your cell phone if you have that feature. This photo will serve as a reference in case your luggage is lost and assist with baggage and insurance claims. Quite often, travelers are very flustered (understandably) when their luggage is misplaced and forget what they actually brought. Frequent travelers taking different bags can add to the confusion.

- Remove all old baggage claim tickets from your bags. Keep them at home in your scrap book. Remember to remove all carry straps from your luggage before checking it. They tend to catch on other objects and are often damaged or missing when you receive your luggage at the other end.

- Make an old fashioned "pom-pom" in a bright color yarn to tie on the handle of your luggage. This makes it more personalized and easier for you to identify it on the baggage carousel and in large groups of bags.

- Spray a large "dot" in the center of your case, using a fluorescent color, and no one will want it!

- To deter thieves and identify your case, use brightly colored surgical or electrical tape in a unique design or your initials.

- Put your initials in the upper right-hand corner of your luggage for added identification. Inexpensive stencils can be purchased. When so many bags look alike, this will help you identify yours.

- Use a luggage strap around the girth of your suitcases to help spot your bag and keep it closed. This is especially helpful on hard sided luggage. Be sure to write your name on it in ink to discourage people from taking it along your travel route.

- For a distinctive luggage tag, try a bone-shaped metal ID tag — found at pet stores. These usually offer more space for information as well.

- Do not put your title on your luggage tag, for example, Dr., Capt., Prof., etc. This increases your chance for theft.

Serious Shopper Tips:

- For major shopping trips, pack a small suitcase with all your items, and then place it inside a large empty suitcase. When you are ready to return home, fill the empty one with your purchases.

- For lots of souvenirs, pack an extra large collapsible bag in your suitcase. On your return trip, fill it up and it becomes a roomy 22" x 18" x 7" bag that's sturdy enough to use as a checked piece of luggage.

- Pack a lightweight nylon zip bag with a shoulder strap for any extra purchases made during the day—and it packs easily. How often have we all needlessly spent money on another bag when our closets are full of them?

- Don't forget compression bags to save even more space on the way home.

Luggage Storage Tips

- Nest luggage (place smaller bags inside larger bags) whenever possible to save space.

- Place crumpled-up newspapers inside luggage to help keep dampness and mildew to a minimum. The paper will absorb the wetness. Change every few months.

- When storing luggage, dampness can be a problem, so putting some small packets of silica gel (that come in shoe boxes) can be very useful to ward away dampness in stored luggage, camera bags, shoe-storage bags, etc.

- If dampness occurs in luggage, use a hair dryer to eliminate it. Also to cut down on dampness, cut a bar of deodorant soap in half and place inside your luggage during storage.

- Cedar shavings or kitty litter are also suggested for stored luggage.

- Place a few dryer sheets inside each bag. This keeps them smelling fresh and clean.

- If your luggage has been stored for quite awhile, place it open in the sunshine to air it out before packing.

- To clean your luggage: Use a small hand vacuum cleaner or whisk broom to clean the inside of your cases. The small size allows you to get into the corners.

- Remove stains from luggage fabric immediately with soap and water to avoid odor. When you return home, the bag can be professionally dry cleaned. Check the manufacturer's label prior to using any cleaning solution. Water-repellent sprays work wonders on soft-sided luggage to prevent stains and keep water from soaking in.

- Spend a few moments finding which keys belong to which suitcases. Once you have them together, use twist ties from the kitchen to secure them to the proper handle.

- Pack off-season clothing inside unused luggage, store in normal room temperature conditions.

Luggage Insurance

There are various ways to insure luggage. Ask your travel agent how much your luggage is insured for by your airline, tour or cruise company you are traveling with. If you are traveling on your own, or are interested in additional luggage insurance, here are some options.

- Inquire about your homeowner's coverage, which generally covers your personal belongings up to an amount stated in your policy, including cameras and luggage.

- Ask your travel agent to recommend a travel insurance policy. They usually have a few to choose from, with varying amounts of coverage at varying fees.

- If you charge your air, tour or cruise tickets to major credit cards, you may be automatically covered, at no extra charge, against loss or significant damage to your baggage. Confirm your card benefits, as they are subject to change.

More Great Tips

- Carry your film in your carry-on baggage. Checked luggage may receive a much more concentrated screening from the high tech scanners, which can ruin film.

- If you are taking a soft sided suitcase, consider putting all your clothing in plastic bags first. You never know when someone else's bag might break and leak perfume all over your bag. Plastic bags are most helpful if your bag is left sitting in the rain along your travels.

- Carry extra keys to your luggage. Combination lock luggage has an advantage over key locks, since you don't have to risk searching for lost keys. As most luggage keys will open luggage of a similar type, ask the hotel or your neighbor for a key if you do forget or lose yours.

- Constantly count your luggage while traveling (including carry-ons, briefcases and purses) to assure that something was not left on the plane, train, bus, taxi, or ship.

- If you're taking sports equipment, musical

instruments or other unique items with you, call your airline in advance to find out if there are any additional charges or special packing instructions/ restrictions.

- Do not check your luggage curbside unless it is absolutely necessary. It is best to take it inside to the counter. The ticket counter has up-to-the minute information of your flight details in case of cancellation or delay.

*"Take half the clothes and
twice the amount of money you
think you'll need."*

Unknown

- 7 -

Planning Your
Travel Wardrobe

Choosing a travel wardrobe of basics will help you deal with space limitations. Build your wardrobe using one or two basic colors, so the same shoes, hosiery and accessories can be worn with everything. Some versatile color combinations are black and red, navy and red, brown and beige or black and white.

Simple, classic styles for dress and casual wear usually work best. Make sure that each item of clothing can be worn at least two ways.

For warmer climates, pack lighter colors and natural fabrics, such as cotton. Unlike synthetics, cotton breathes. For cooler climates, dark colored clothing, which can be layered for warmth, is a good choice. Wool gabardine is a good fabric to travel with as it's lightweight, warm and wrinkle resistant.

One of my favorite travel items is a pair of khaki pants because they're the color of — dirt! By wearing dark colors on the bottom, like khaki and black, you don't have to worry about dirt showing when you sit on a park bench or on a train seat. The best thing about khaki is that any color in the world matches it. That takes out half the stress of planning what to wear! And, depending on my destination, I also travel with Capri pants or a longer length skirt which helps me blend in and be more culturally sensitive in certain areas of the world.

One clothing question I'm asked more than any other is, "How do you pack for changing climates especially when you're starting out in, say, Scandinavia and ending your trip in Greece?" The secret is layering. You can take items off as you get hot and layer them back on as you get cold.

The answer for travelers who tend to get cold easily is lightweight long underwear. Available in two piece sets (nylon/cotton or silk) they fit well under any type of clothing. They're easy to pack, drip dry overnight and keep you warm. You can even use them for pajamas.

For plane travel, wear loose-fitting clothing with elastic waistbands and comfortable rubber soled shoes for walking long distances in airports. Wear a short sleeved shirt under a long sleeved sweater so if you are arriving to a warmer climate than which you left, you can simply take off the layers as needed.

Don't forget what you are wearing is an additional outfit to the clothes that you have packed, so make sure these items mix and match with your packed clothes.

Organizing your wardrobe is easier if you have a list of things that you plan to take with you. Keep the list of items in your carry-on bag. If checked bags are misplaced, the list of contents can help identify them.

I pack almost the same amount of clothes for a one week trip as I do for a three week trip. I just wash along the way (see page 91). Who wants to carry their entire closet around on vacation?

Shoes

Shoes are always a hot topic. Throughout the years, I've found there are "shoe people" in this world who travel with every pair of shoes they own. If you're one of them, and you just can't convert, be sure you have someone available to help you carry your bags!

My suggestion is to travel with a maximum of 3 pairs of shoes, one that you're wearing and two that you pack. My preference is a good walking shoe, a comfortable dressy loafer and a pair of sandals. Modify your shoes depending on your destination and be sure to break in any new shoes before leaving home. And flip flops take little room and are a good choice for many reasons, so I always toss in a pair for all my travels.

For longer trips and cruises, a few additional pair of shoes is usually warranted. I generally suggest adding a dressier pair of shoes and a tennis/sport shoe to the basic three already mentioned.

One of my favorite shoe stories is from a cruise I was on. I was flown to Australia to demonstrate at the end of a world cruise how to "Pack It All Up and Get it home." Realize that the passengers had been onboard for over 100 days. I mentioned during my demonstration that I recommend a maximum of 3 pair of shoes if you're trying to pack light, and a passenger came up to me at the end of the talk. She said she'd been on board the entire time and had 47 pairs of shoes with her. Having lived aboard ships for years, I was familiar with the size of most cabins, and you'd be hard pressed to fit 47 pairs of shoes in most cabins. When I asked her were she kept all her shoes, she replied, "Oh Anne, I just bought the cabin next door and used it for my closet!" Now, if you can travel that way, I say take as many shoes as you'd like! However, most of us don't travel like that.

Don't forget to pack rubber-soled shoes when traveling to places with cobblestone streets and marble floors, where it's easy to slip and fall.

Jewelry

I can't stress this tip enough: Leave your good jewelry safe at home in a locked safety deposit box and take only inexpensive jewelry you can wear without worry. Faux pearls make a very elegant statement and look just as nice as real ones without the worry.

How to pack a necklace so it doesn't get kinks in it: thread it through a straw (cut to the length of the necklace and/or bracelet) and then close the clasp. Place in a travel toothbrush holder so it won't be crushed in your luggage. Pack inside a shoe for further protection.

- Pack pierced earrings in a lipstick container so they don't get crushed (or use an empty film canister or prescription pill bottle).

- Pack your jewelry in a mini-size, double-sided tackle box when traveling. The individual compartments (which can be lined with skid proof shelf lining) work great for earrings and rings. In the longer compartments, put straight pins in the shelf lining at an angle then loop your necklaces around the pins so the chains don't get tangled.

- If you must take valuables with you, be sure to store them in a hotel/ship safe.

On the next two pages you'll find the Women's and

Men's Travel Wardrobe List to get you started. Modify each accordingly, depending on the type of travel that you are doing.

Women's Basic Travel Wardrobe
❏ Walking shoes
❏ Flat loafers
❏ Sandals (if appropriate)
❏ Dress shoes (if appropriate)
❏ Socks
❏ Underwear
❏ Hosiery/Slip
❏ Pajamas
❏ 2 pair of pants, one light, one dark
❏ 2 belts (one in each basic color)
❏ Skirt
❏ Jacket to match pants and skirt
❏ Lightweight sweater
❏ Shorts (if appropriate)
❏ 3 short sleeved knit t-shirts
❏ 2 long sleeved knit t-shirt
❏ Evening blouse
❏ Dress (if appropriate)
❏ Swimsuit/ Sarong
❏ Costume jewelry
❏ Scarf
❏ Raincoat
❏ Hat/gloves (if appropriate)
❏ Travel umbrella (if appropriate)
❏ Athletic wear (if appropriate)
❏ Convertible handbag = day into evening

Men's Basic Travel Wardrobe

❏ Walking shoes
❏ Sandals
❏ Loafers or dress shoes
❏ Underpants
❏ Undershirts
❏ Socks (casual)
❏ Socks (dress)
❏ 2 pair pants (khaki and dark)
❏ Shorts
❏ 2 long sleeved shirts
❏ 3 Short sleeved shirts (polo and t-shirts)
❏ V-neck or crew neck sweater
❏ Sport coat
❏ Necktie (if appropriate)
❏ 2 belts
❏ Sleepwear
❏ Overcoat
❏ Travel umbrella
❏ Pair swim trunks (if appropriate)
❏ Hat/gloves (if appropriate)
❏ Athletic wear (if appropriate)

Travel Wardrobe Planner

The key to an organized travel wardrobe is planning. A few weeks before your trip, start a list of clothing you'd like to take. Match each piece to a day of travel, then figure out what can be mixed and matched to cut down on what you take. Remember, you can wear each item at least a few times, especially black pants and khaki capris. On page 59 you'll find one of my favorite secrets, my **Travel Wardrobe Planner**. I've used this for years and it really works to help cut back on the number of clothes I pack. I started using it for cruises and now I use it for every trip. Please see page 108 for the **Cruise Wardrobe Planner**.

To help you get started: Add or subtract days on the planner depending on the length of your trip. Write down an outfit for day and night and decide how often you can wear the same things again. Be sure to write down the separate pieces, i.e. black skirt, red blouse, to remind you that separates can be mixed and matched and worn more than one time. Separates stretch your travel wardrobe further than a single item like a dress. You'll be amazed at how much less you'll really need to take (and how much money you can save on things you probably won't wear or need).

Note any events and activities you'll be participating in so you have the appropriate clothing.

Please feel free to make copies so you have extra planners ready for future trips.

Tips

- Remember to take items that can double for other uses. A raincoat can act as a blanket on a train or bus. A large t-shirt can be used for a nightgown, exercising or cover-up.

- Don't overlook the need for some real casual clothes like your favorite sweats, t-shirts and tennis shoes. These are great for relaxing around the hotel room, exercising or for long traveling days.

- When traveling for a special event (i.e. wedding, etc.) or within different climates on one trip, pack the clothing, shoes, etc. that are no longer needed and mail them back home.

AM FAVE

Don't forget to pack some dryer sheets. Rub them against clothing to reduce static. In dry climates, you can rub your comb across them to reduce static in your hair (or even rub them on your head)! Packed in your luggage, they can make your clothes smell nice. Be sure not to use on silk items, though.

- You can bring less with you if you plan to purchase some of your wardrobe along the way in the form of souvenir t-shirts and sweatshirts. Be certain that you save enough room in your luggage to bring them home. See shopping tips page 45.

- Convertible clothing extends your travel wardrobe options without the added weight of another piece of clothing. Convertible pants zip-off to make an extra pair of shorts and a fleece jacket with zip off sleeves converts to a vest in case the weather warms up.

- Reversible clothing also stretches your travel wardrobe by giving you two items in one. Check **www.packitup.com** for some great ideas like jackets and skirts.

- Pack some clothes that are on their last legs i.e. underwear or a sweater that's quite worn. During your travels, leave them behind with a note in your hotel room explaining that you've meant to leave them. And you've made space for some souvenirs!

Pack It Up—Travel Wardrobe Planner

	City	Daytime Outfit	Evening Outfit	Special Events & Activities
Day 1				
Day 2				
Day 3				
Day 4				
Day 5				
Day 6				
Day 7				

©Pack It Up

"He who would travel happily must travel light."

Antoine De Saint-Exupery

- 8 -
Pack It In

Packing wisely can avoid unnecessary problems and save expenses. Be sure to pack lightly, and only pack luggage you can carry or wheel for one mile without putting down!

Always start with a checklist. To save you time, please see page 164 for the Ultimate Traveler's Checklist. This checklist covers just about everything you might possibly *need* for any trip. It is not a checklist of everything you should *take* for every trip.

This list will serve as a helpful reminder of what you might need. It will speed up packing, let you know what you might be missing and help you eliminate items you won't need.

The last thing any traveler wants is to buy something on their trip (usually at a greater expense) that they have sitting at home. Feel free to tear out this checklist and make as many copies as you need. You can also download it at **www.packitup.com**.

Packing Your Carry-On Bags

Most airlines allow one personal bag and one carry-on bag. Always confirm in advance with your specific airline what is allowed and the specific sizes of each bag. Generally, a personal bag is defined as a purse, briefcase, small backpack or laptop computer bag. A carry-on bag is the larger of the two items. Confirm what size your airline will allow.

At least one of the items should be stowed under the seat in front of you. If you are traveling on more than one airline, be sure to check with the other airlines for their specific baggage rules as rules vary from airline to airline.

As mentioned in the "Luggage Tips" in chapter 6, I suggest traveling with a 16" rolling tote. Since, by the time you pack everything you need into your carry-on, it can be incredibly heavy.

You should also pack a collapsible tote bag in your rolling tote. The benefit of having the additional bag is if the airline won't permit you to carry-on your rolling tote, you can transfer the important items from this bag to your tote bag and check the larger rolling tote bag. You'll also have an extra bag for packing souvenirs for the trip home.

In the following two checklists, you'll notice that items are divided into 1) most important in your personal bag and 2) less important in your carry-on bag. If you have to check your carry-on bag at the last minute (this can happen on smaller aircraft), everything you need will still be accessible under the seat in front of you. The only guaranteed space you have on a plane is the space beneath the seat in front of you (and sometimes that is limited due to seat configuration and bulkhead seats do not have any space at all).

Remember to pack as many items as possible in your carry-on in plastic bags. This makes everything easier to identify, and you can efficiently transfer valuable items in a hurry so they are with you all times. (see pages 79 for plastic bag ideas)

Most importantly, if you are traveling on business or for

a special occasion and you must be dressed appropriately, be sure to either wear what you need or carry it on the plane with you. No worries over delayed luggage.

If traveling with a security wallet, please refer to the checklist on page 32 for a list of items to be kept in your security wallet.

Carry-on Checklists:

Carry-on Personal Bag (most important items)

Pack your handbag/purse inside this personal tote bag, allowing you extra room for the following items:

❏ Document organizer including:
- Travel documents/Photo ID
- Credit cards/Cash
❏ Medications
❏ Quart-size Plastic Bag w/liquids
❏ Jewelry
❏ Camera/film/memory card
❏ Computer
❏ Business files
❏ Cell phone and charger
❏ Eye glasses/sunglasses
❏ Keys
❏ Address book
❏ Healthy snack and water
❏ Tissues
❏ Comfort items (please see page 69)

Carry-on Rolling Tote Bag (less important items)

❏ Extra reading material

❏ Make-up/toothbrush and paste

❏ Change of underwear/socks/shirt

❏ Any item from above list that's not vital to you

❏ Expandible tote bag (that you can pull out and transfer some of these items in case you need to check your rolling tote bag)

Packing Your Suitcase

Inter-layering is what I call the following method of packing luggage. It is the most successful method for preventing wrinkles in your clothes. Begin with your suitcase open on a flat surface.

1. Place your shoes in pairs with the toe-tucked-in the heel method inside plastic bags. Put your shoes and all heavy items along the bottom of the suitcase (near the hinges). Place belts along the perimeter of the case and heavy items, such as hair dryer, cosmetic case, etc. in the center.

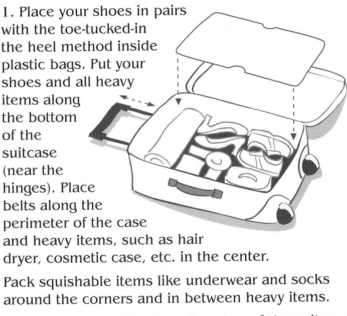

Pack squishable items like underwear and socks around the corners and in between heavy items.

Now, place a packing board on top of these items.

If you don't have one, you can use an over-sized placemat.

The benefit of a packing board is that it provides a flat packing surface for your clothing.

2. Fold your slacks along their natural creases and place the waistband against one edge of your suit-case with the bot-tom of the pant extending over the opposite edge of the case.

Place the second pair of slacks in the same method in the opposite direction.

3. Continue folding your skirts and dresses along their natural creases and use the "In-terlayering" technique of layer-ing each article in the opposite direc-tion until all your slacks, skirts, and dresses are packed.

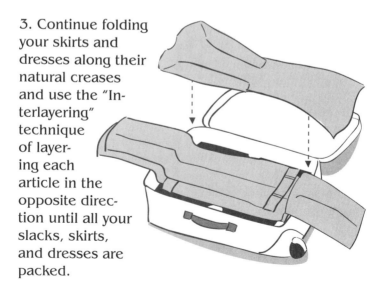

4. Next, button all jackets, blazers, and long sleeved shirts and pull a dry-cleaner bag over them. Place them in the suitcase with the sleeves being brought in on top of the jacket along their natural creases. The bottom of these items will extend over the top edge of the case.

5. Roll up all knit items and place them on top of the layered clothing, leaving the original articles extended over the edges of the case. Make sure you utilized every inch of space so items will not slip during travel.

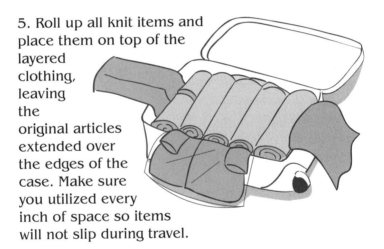

6. When you have utilized every inch of space, bring the ends up and over the rolled items inside the case, alternating sides as you go. This keeps your clothing in a continuous rounded shape without getting wrinkles at the knee caps of the slacks and jacket waistlines. It is also easier to pull out certain items you may need without disturbing the entire case of clothes.

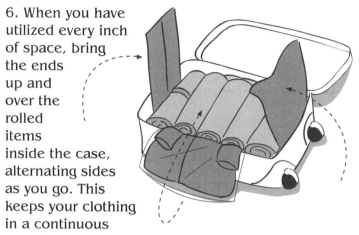

When all items are packed, another benefit of the packing board is: You can reach in and lift out your top layer of clothes without disturbing them and retrieve items on the bottom layer.

For information on Anne's Packing Board, visit: **www.packitup.com**

How To Roll Up a T-shirt:

1. Place your t-shirt on a flat surface

2. Fold sleeves to each other

3. Roll up from the bottom.

Remember, the tighter you roll your knits, the less they wrinkle.

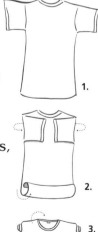

67

Additional Hints For Packing Your Suitcase

- Begin packing with a variety of plastic bags next to your bag. Everything that's possible to pack in a bag, do. This keeps items more organized and you have extra bags ready if you need them while traveling.

- Pack all of your heavy items (hair dryer, shoes, electrical converter, etc.) on the bottom of your bag. Stuff your shoes with socks, hose, underwear, anything that won't wrinkle easily.

- An oldie but a goodie: Place tissue paper between folds to reduce wrinkles.

- For packing pleated skirts, turn them inside out, wrap masking tape around the hem (to keep the pleats set), and pull into an old pair of panty hose with the top and bottom cut off. This will keep the pleats in and the skirt from wrinkling. Place around the perimeter of case.

- To organize your outfits and reduce wrinkles, roll your knit separates together.

- Sweaters are easy to roll up, usually don't wrinkle, and fit well into the corners, keeping other items from shifting in your suitcase.

- When using dry-cleaner bags, make sure the bags do not have anything printed on them (i.e. advertising). The ink can rub off on clothing when it gets warm.

- Turn all sequin items or embroidered clothes inside out and place in either a plastic bag or pillowcase to minimize rubbing and loosening sequins. (This also allows you to have your own pillowcase on your trip.)

- Pack your jewelry in your evening bag so you know exactly where it is.

- Stuff all the corners in your luggage with small, soft items to save space: socks, underwear, hose, and all things that won't wrinkle.

- Fold blouses and men's shirts inside out so the wrinkles are facing inside and not so prominent.

- Place items that you intend to use first on the top of your suitcase: shorts, bathing suit, pajamas, etc.

 When packing a bathing suit with cups (or bras) the cups can get crushed. Pack a pair of socks in the cups to keep them filled out. Roll-up and place in a plastic bag to avoid snags.

- The contents of a suitcase will settle, leaving more space for additional items if packed the day before departure. Pre-packing allows peace of mind and time to clear out the refrigerator!

- Place men's cuff links and studs in plastic or felt containers and put in jacket pockets. If valuable, pack in your carry-on.

Comfort Items (not just for planes anymore)

A few "must haves" for every carry-on bag: A healthy snack and a bottle of water. As the saying goes, "You never know when your next meal is coming." Inflatable neck and lumbar pillows and earplugs and eyeshades also provide an extra touch of comfort on the plane. (Tip: Most airlines no longer provide pillows and blankets so be prepared to take your own).

Compression Bags

In addition to keeping all of your items organized, clean and protected, reusable compression bags will also seal in odors and moisture, so they're great for dirty laundry on the way home. Packing bulky items like sweaters in these bags can create up to 75% more space in your bag. (Remember you can also add a great deal of weight to your bag so be careful how many compression bags you use!)

Step 1. Packing a Compression Bag

Make sure all articles are folded neatly before placing them in the bag. Make sure all pins or sharp objects are removed from clothing. Slide items into bag.

Step 2. Closing the Zipper

Squeeze sealer and slide from one end to the other. Ensure the zipper is completely closed by zipping it back and forth a few times.

Step 3. Compressing Articles in the Bag

You can either roll or press straight down on the bag to compress and release excess air. To compress by rolling,

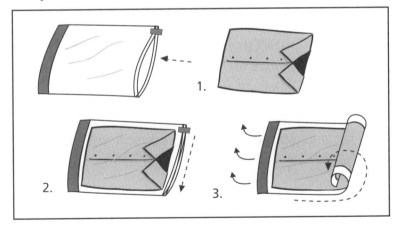

start at the zipper end and roll towards the valve end. Hold onto packed articles as you roll, keeping them away from the valve end. To help prevent wrinkling, press straight down on wrinkle sensitive items, rather than roll them.

I realized I couldn't travel without compression bags after my trip to Peru. I was packing for both business and vacation and didn't think I had room for both my fleece jacket and raincoat. So I packed them each into a medium size compression bag, squished out the air, and packed them in my small carry-on bag. Now I always take 2 compression bags packed with bulky items and 2 extras for laundry on the way home.

Packing Folders and Cubes

Packing folders and cubes are another great way to organize your items. Folders work well for packing shirts, blouses and pants. Pack a day's worth of clothing inside each folder to keep it wrinkle free and easy to inspect. Great for car travel and for organizing large duffle bags where items tend to get lost at the bottom of the bag. Packing cubes are great for organizing small, easy-to-lose pieces of clothing like socks. For more information on both folders and cubes visit: **www.packitup.com**.

Packing Your Garment Bag

There are many different types and sizes of garment bags on the market. Some have built-in frames and some are simply heavy material designed to cover your clothes. Depending on the specific type of garment bag you have, the following suggestions will assist in packing it more successfully for your next trip.

When packing your garment bag, use a maximum number of three hangers. Begin by placing your garment bag on a flat surface. Next, layer your clothes on the hangers in the following methods:

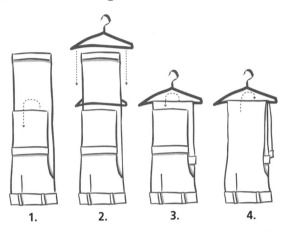

1. Place pants on a flat surface and fold top pant leg back in half

2. Slip hanger on bottom pant leg to knee

3. Fold bottom of pant leg to crotch over the hanger

4. Fold top pant leg over the hanger and over the other pant leg

This secures the pants to the hanger so they don't slip off.

(also great for RV travel, car travel, and your home closet!)

1. After securing pants as described, place shirts (buttoning articles as you go along) over the pants and ultimately jackets.

1.

Cover each hanger with dry-cleaner bags once all the clothes have been hung on it.

2. Place dresses on the next hanger and cover them with dry-cleaner bags helping to protect them and keep wrinkles to a minimum.

3. After you have all your clothes on the hangers, place your coat (or robe) around all of the clothing, and button it up.

2.   **3.**

Place bundled hanging items inside your garment bag.

Gently fold any garments up at the bottom if they are longer than the garment bag. Secure the strap of the garment bag around the center of the "bundle" if provided.

In the additional packing area around the hangers, stuff the corners with either socks or shoes or knit clothes that have been rolled up. Be sure to pad high-heeled shoes or any sharp items so as not to poke through the bag. Remember, any sharp items must be packed in your checked bag.

The biggest mistake most people make when

73

packing garment bags is they don't pack enough to keep items from shifting and everything falls to the bottom of the bag.

Additional Hints for Packing A Garment Bag

- Use rubber bands to keep hangers together if they are not those that originally came with the bag. This will keep them from falling and snagging clothes on the way down.

- Place those garments that wrinkle easily at the back of the bag (closest to the outside). In this way, they will have less pressure and be less likely to wrinkle. Don't over-pack your garment bag or it will be very cumbersome to carry.

- Don't forget luggage straps that are used mainly around the girth of hard sided luggage. These are terrific to keep your garment bag together, especially when you're carrying it.

- Be sure to secure the hook of your bag by zipping it into the pocket provided.

- Place plastic cable ties on your checked garment bag zippers to help keep them closed. Pack a pair of fingernail clippers in one of the outside unzipped pockets to remove the cable ties.

- When carrying your garment bag on the plane, make sure to keep it near your seat. Tri-fold garment bags are much easier to fit in the overhead compartment (and through security check points).

- Don't pack valuables in your garment bag in case it is moved out of sight.

Packing A Duffel Bag

When traveling by car, duffels are a great way to organize, especially for family travel. However, it is one of the most difficult bags to pack, unless you know the secrets.

First, always pack a duffel bag on a hard surface. This will help distribute the weight evenly. Pack your duffel in layers with the heaviest items on the bottom, such as shoes, sandals, extra travel guides and umbrella.

Next, nestle your toiletry kit on top of your shoes, which will help protect the contents in case it's dropped.

Pack your clothes as previously instructed for a suitcase using a packing board. Place the board on a flat surface like your bed, not inside your duffel. Layer your clothes on top of the divider just like the suitcase packing, and when you're finished, pick up the entire bundle and place it inside your duffel bag.

Next, stuff your socks, underwear, swim suit, etc. all around the edges of the duffel and remember to never pack anything breakable in a duffel bag.

Fill-in corners with sweaters and bulky items rolled-up. This protects the items on the inside of the duffel, and allows you to pack more.

Other options for packing clothing in a duffel bag are packing folders and cubes. Build your layers with the folders and cubes on top of the bottom layer of shoes.

Finally, pack your rain jacket and pajamas on top next to the zipper, in case they're needed in a hurry. The outside pockets of duffel bags are perfect for packing extra plastic bags and other non-breakable items.

General Packing Tips

- First, make a list of all the items that you want to take with you as you think of them. Check off these items as you pack. Keep this packing list and use it as a reference for your next trip.

- Another idea is to list all the activities you will be attending while you are away. Then list what clothes and accessories you need. Start by laying out your items on an extra bed or couch as you think of them.

- Inter-pack your luggage with your traveling companion. In case one piece is missing or delayed, you will still have a few items of your own. This idea also applies to traveling alone and "scattering" your casual and formal clothes between your various cases. Some may find this impractical, but it works!

- If you run out of plastic bags on your way home, use the free shower cap as a shoe cover (works great on large mens shoes).

 Women's shoes pack neatly inside men's shoes. This saves space and the women's shoes are nicely protected. Pack socks and hose inside women's shoe, place women's shoe inside a plastic bag, and then slide women's shoe into man's.

- Place shoes inside the plastic bag that newspapers come in. They are long and perfect for large shoes. Since they are clear, you can see what's inside. Plastic bags from sub sandwich shops also work great!

- Before you start packing, place the clothes you think you'll need on your bed, then place half of them back in the closet.

• When in doubt, leave it out!

• Only pack luggage you can carry or wheel around your block without putting it down or stopping. This gives you a good idea of what you will encounter on your travels and what you can handle by yourself.

• If you're pressed for space, wear your heaviest clothing instead of packing it.

• Don't forget the old trick of hanging wrinkled items in a bathroom full of steam to help refresh them.

• Pack paper back books you plan to read around the edge of your suitcase for extra protection. Lighten your load by giving them away before your trip home.

• Be sure to pack an outfit in your carry-on bag. If the worst happens and your checked bag is delayed, you don't have to run out in the middle of the night looking for clothes in a foreign city. Consider this your survival kit.

• Leave clothes on wire hangers from the dry cleaner and pack them in your large checked suitcase. When you unpack for an extended stay, simply lift out the hangers and your clothes are ready to go into the closet.

• Save the inserts of perfume and cologne samples from magazines to use when traveling. You won't have to worry about bottles breaking.

• Place dryer sheets in between the layers of your clothes. This helps avoid static cling and keeps everything smelling fresh. You'll then have some dryer sheets if you need them for laundry on the road.

• The more your travel, the less you take.

"*The only aspect of our travels
that is guaranteed to hold an audience
is disaster.*"

Martha Gellman

- 9 -
Plastic Bags to The Rescue

Out of the kitchen and into your bag, don't leave home without Ziploc® bags. Since my first trip to Europe, and 67 countries later, my favorite packing essential is still the plastic bag. They are see-through and help prevent leaks. And, best of all, they are affordable to replace for each trip.

Before I actually start packing my bags, I first put everything possible inside plastic bags. The see-through feature of packing in plastic makes finding things simple. And the wide variety of sizes—snack, quart, gallon and big bags — allows me to keep the things I want together, regardless of how big or small.

Plastic bags are great for separating wet items, like swimsuits and exercise clothes, and the large sizes are perfect for laundry that you don't want to think about until you get home.

Don't forget to pack extras for use along the way and the trip home: Make your own "soft pack" of varying sizes of plastic bags to travel with. Pack quart and snack size bags inside a gallon bag and pack gallon bags inside Ziploc® Big Bags. Roll up and secure with a rubber band or pack flat on the bottom of your bag. Distribute extra bags throughout your luggage: inside your toiletry kit, in the outside pockets of your carry-on, inside luggage pockets, etc. You'll find uses for them everywhere. Even pack one in your coat pocket — just in case!

Airport Organization with Plastic Bags

Security Organizer

As mentioned in "Packing Smart for Airport Security," first, pack everything in your carry-on in plastic bags, if possible. This will this help expedite your trip through security because they're see-through and help organize your bag. And why not make it as pleasant as possible for security personnel: Keep personal items like underwear inside a plastic bag.

Here's a tip: Start emptying your pockets before you get up to the security check point. Keep a plastic bag in your carry-on for just this purpose.

Sharps!

Write "Sharps" on the outside of a quart size bag so you remember to pack everything together that isn't permitted in your carry-on bag. Always pack this bag in your checked-in bag. (Your pocket knife, cork screw, etc.) Check tsa.gov for an updated list of permitted items.

Film

Always place your film inside a plastic bag before you pack it in your carry-on bag. This will help expedite the screening process if you request a hand inspection of your film at security. (The bag allows the inspector to view the canisters easily.) Be sure to arrive early to avoid long lines and remember: Never pack film in your checked luggage. Equipment used for screening checked baggage might damage your undeveloped film.

Valuable Bag

Keep valuables (or any necessary items like medicine) together in a plastic bag you can pull from your carry-on, should you have to check your carry-on at the last minute.

 Keep all your items close at hand on the plane by organizing them in a "plane pocket." Pack everything you'll need on your plane trip inside a gallon size bag: Healthy snack, comfort items, iPod®, medication, pens and paper, ear plugs, paperback, glasses etc. and place in the seat pocket in front of you. Easy access and you won't loose items as easily.

Healthy Food on The Go

You can take it with you, so why not? Fill-up some small snack size bags with healthy snacks for your trip. Here are some ideas: Dried cranberries, beef jerky, mixed nuts, energy bars, carrots and celery and trail mix. Combined with a small bottle of water, you've got a meal on the go. Most flights no longer provide food so be prepared. For more travel friendly food ideas and recipes, including my favorite Panforte, go to **www.packitup.com**.

More Great Travel Tips with Plastic Bags
Scrapbook Organizer — Travel Memories

AM FAVE

When traveling to numerous countries on one trip, write each country (i.e. Italy) on the front of a gallon size bag and organize your mementos accordingly. When you return home, it's a breeze to put your scrapbook in order. Toss in your souvenir coins, museum tickets (some are works of art), brochures and postcards in the correct "country."

Personal Care Organizers
Arrive at your destination organized by grouping your personal care items by category inside plastic bags. Pack all the items you use in the shower like shampoo, conditioner, soap, razor, etc. in a gallon size bag and mark the outside "shower." For items you use by the bed, like alarm clock, lotion, tissues, write "bed" on the bag. Make a few "sink" bags, one containing make-up and cotton swabs, one containing deodorant, facial cleanser, moisturizer, and yet another containing your toothbrush, toothpaste and floss. Pack all these bags inside your hanging toiletry kit (packed with your brush, etc.) for traveling.

Travel Make-up Kit
Always pack each liquid cosmetic item that might leak inside a plastic bag. Keep a box of snack size bags in your bathroom cupboard handy for every time you pack your makeup. If your foundation leaks en route, it won't ruin your expensive blush. Pack all cosmetics inside a large plastic bag to keep them organized.

Comfort on the Go

After a long day of travel (or sightseeing), you might have a few sore muscles. Soak a wash cloth in warm water and place inside a plastic bag to make a hot compress. Alternatively, make a cold compress by placing ice in a bag. To avoid leaks, double-up your bags. The hot compress idea also works well as a hot water bottle in a pinch—place in your bed a few minutes before retiring to warm up your sheets!

Car Organization

Organize everything from your glove compartment to your trunk with extra strong plastic bags. Pack maps, flashlight, etc. and keep close at hand. Keep your insurance card, car ID, etc. all together in a quart size bag, just in case. Keep children's small snacks, games, and drawing supplies all together in a gallon bag in the backseat pocket, within their reach.

Use large bags to keep awkward sized items like jumper cables contained. For winter weather, keep one packed with gloves, hat and socks. For summer, keep one packed with sunscreen, extra bathing suit and sun hat (one for each child). These fit easily under the front seats. See page 123 for more car tips.

Luggage/Clothing Organization

Gallon size bags are great for children's clothing. Pack an entire day's worth of clothes inside a gallon bag and write each child's name on the outside. This is a great way to organize a duffle bag or a suitcase, too. The large bags work well for adult-sized items like bulky sweaters, coats and shoes (and you can also pack a day's worth of clothes inside).

Directions: Fold the items an inch smaller than the

83

bag and stack on top of each other. Then, slide the entire stack of clothes into the bag on a flat surface and press ALL air out of the bag. Close zipper until one inch remains open. Press remaining air out of the bag and zip the bag all the way closed. Toss it in your suitcase. This makes a very flat package taking up less room in your luggage. To reduce wrinkles and save space, try to remove as much air as possible and flatten with your hands.

Travel Washing Machine

Save money on laundry by turning a plastic bag into a washing machine. See AM FAVE on page 93.

Garbage Bags

Grab a few large garbage bags from under your kitchen sink before heading out on your next trip. From a drop cloth for a picnic to an impromptu rain poncho, you'll be prepared. If it's raining, cover your luggage or line the inside of your luggage to protect your clothing from rain.

Compression Bags

The ultimate plastic bag, the compression bag is great for a variety of items. My favorite use is for dirty laundry. Since they seal-in odors and moisture, they're also great for wet swimsuits and damp workout gear. They are also wonderful for packing fleece jackets, sweaters, and entire outfits. And, for anyone who likes to travel with their own pillow, you can actually pack a full size pillow into a large compression bag and shrink it down to less than 1". Please see page 70.

- 10 -
Packing Your Toiletries

For many, packing toiletries and other personal care items can be the most challenging part of packing. Deciding exactly what to take and figuring out how to prevent leaks can be difficult.

The first place to start is to use a good toiletry kit. Just in case something leaks, separate your personal care items from everything else in your bag. You'll need this bag to be multi-functional, so it fits any type of travel you're planning.

My hanging toiletry kit has traveled the world with me and suits my needs well. I've used the same one for over 10 years, for 5 star cruises to trekking in Nepal. The reason I like it so much is the hook allows me to hang the bag on any door handle, shower rod or towel rack - a great benefit when there's limited counter space.

It's large enough for all my toiletries, including shampoo, conditioner, hair brush, toothbrush/paste, etc. It also has a non-breakable mirror.

Be sure to pack your toiletries one to two days in advance and then go through your normal routine. Check to make sure everything you need is ready to go. Remember that travel sizes of everything conserve space.

More great tips for organizing your personal care items:

- If you go on frequent trips, keep your toiletry kit packed so you're always ready to go.

- To help prepare for your next trip: Keep a list of items that are running low inside your toiletry kit when you're traveling. When you return, stock the bag relying on your list to prepare for the next trip. Then all you have to do is grab it out of the closet and go. No need for that mad dash to the store for last minute items.

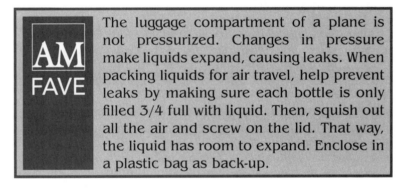

The luggage compartment of a plane is not pressurized. Changes in pressure make liquids expand, causing leaks. When packing liquids for air travel, help prevent leaks by making sure each bottle is only filled 3/4 full with liquid. Then, squish out all the air and screw on the lid. That way, the liquid has room to expand. Enclose in a plastic bag as back-up.

- Place a small piece of plastic wrap over bottle lids before closing. This keeps the liquid from spilling.

- Purchase leak-proof plastic bottles at luggage stores or travel catalogs. These are much better than the empty plastic bottles found at drug stores which often leak. Nalgene® bottles are the favorite of experienced travelers.

- Bottles with a spray pump never really seal completely and may leak. Remove the spray pump and transfer the liquid to a leak proof bottle, bringing the travel sized spray pump bottle separately. Assemble once you're at your destination.

- Contact lens wearers should carry their spare glasses, a lens case and a small bottle of saline with them in their carry-on, as long flights can dry and irritate the eyes.

- Shop periodically for travel-size items you may eventually need, and put them away for an upcoming trip. No need to spend time decanting large bottles into small ones.

- In a pinch, use lather from shampoo in place of shaving cream.

- On your travels, collect samples like shampoo and soap from hotel rooms and bring them home, even if not to your taste. Package them up in a small cosmetic bag (like the free ones from the cosmetic counter sales) and give them to a friend for a bon voyage gift. Alternately, keep them for visiting guests to your home or donate to a local shelter.

- Leave your perfume bottle at home and take an inexpensive travel atomizer. Here's a tip: You can take a second atomizer and put vermouth in it for your martinis!

- For the ultra organized, divide your personal care items by category and pack them inside plastic bags before you pack them in your toiletry kit. See page 82.

Packing Your Cosmetics Bag

- Most importantly, never pack your make-up inside your toiletry kit. In case of leakage, you don't want it to ruin expensive makeup. Keep your make-up in a separate zippered bag (I like one that's brightly colored, so it's easy to locate in a black bag).

- Place each item inside a small re-sealable plastic bag just in case something leaks.

- Cut a piece of plastic the same size as your face powder container and place it in the top. This prevents the powder from spilling when you open it.

- Small cosmetic bags with zippers make great places to keep costume jewelry, different currencies, and other small items.

- Invest in one of the all-in-one cosmetic creams, the kind that serves as day moisturizer, night cream, and under-eye cream. This eliminates the need to carry three different items.

- Cosmetics can take up a lot of room so ask at the cosmetic counter for a sample of foundation in the color that you usually use. This should last at least 5 days.

- Use a combination shampoo/conditioner instead of taking two bottles.

- Instead of taking a bottle of fingernail polish remover, which would create a disaster if spilled, pack pre-moistened polish remover pads in plastic baggie.

- Consider traveling with make-up removal pads. These can be used when water is not readily available and are disposable.

- Powdered mineral-based make-up is a good alternative to liquid foundation for the obvious reason: no leaks. Look for powder with SPF protection.

Medical Matters

- Take a list of your medications with you.

- Also, keep a list in your wallet of the medications that you can't take, i.e. the medicines you are allergic to.

- Keep a Medic Alert card in your wallet or purse if you have a medical problem or allergies. It is also advisable to put your blood type on it.

- Update any prescriptions and take extra with you. Be sure to keep all medicine in their original, labeled bottles to avoid problems.

- Since many prescriptions come in large quantities, ask your pharmacist (or mail order pharmacy) to give you the smallest bottles available for your trip. Always take a few extra days of medication in case your trip is unexpectedly extended.

Check **www.tsa.gov** for updated information on traveling with medicine and medical needs.

- Pack a small collapsible cup for taking medication.

- Ask your doctor about traveling with Pepto Bismol® to ease upset stomach, nausea and diarrhea. Many travelers won't leave home without it.

If you have allergic reactions to certain foods, have someone write on a card, in the language of the countries that you are visiting, the foods you cannot eat.

- For muscle relaxation, pack a few air-activated heat wraps in your bag. Just open the pouch and the single-use wrap begins to warm up when exposed to air.

- Pack a dental repair kit for emergencies.

- Include bottled water into your travel budget. Avoid possible stomach problems by only drinking bottled water, especially in exotic areas where the hygiene is questionable. Check that the bottle seal is unopened. You can drink local water if it's been boiled and remember, even the ice cubes in your drink may not have been made out of boiled water. It's worth the extra money. Bottled drinks, such as wine, beer and carbonated drinks are also usually safe.

- Consider packing some refreezable ice cubes which safely chill drinks anywhere the water is "questionable."

- Avoid fresh fruits and vegetables which might have been washed in contaminated water. Peeled fruit is usually safe.

- Carry some pre-packaged peanut butter crackers on long trips. They provide protein and carbohydrates when you can't find a meal that suits your taste.

- Remember to pack a pair of extra reading glasses or spare contacts. If glasses get damaged, it may be difficult to replace them, especially in foreign countries.

- Pack antibacterial wipes for a quick clean up before meals and after you've experienced a restroom on the road. Also great for wiping tray tables and arm rests, hotel remote controls, phones, rental car steering wheels, etc.

- 11 -
Laundry On The Go

I've discovered from polling my audiences over the years that it's about even: 50% of travelers do laundry along the road, and 50% don't. A true vacation for many means no laundry. Options are 1) pay someone to do it for you 2) pack enough clothes to last the entire trip. For some, it's worth the extra money to have someone do it for them. If you're one of them, you can skip this chapter.

The other-half follow the philosophy of doing laundry along the way instead of using expensive hotel laundry services. By washing-out a few items along the way, you can pack lighter. This not only saves money, but it saves valuable vacation time. Who wants to spend a day at the laundromat if you don't have to?

If you're still with me, here's what I do:

Home Made Laundry Kit

Pack the following items in a gallon size plastic bag:

- ❏ Braided Elastic Laundry Line
- ❏ Rubber Sink Stopper
- ❏ Concentrated Travel Laundry Soap
- ❏ Inflatable Hangers
- ❏ Micro-fiber Travel Towel
- ❏ Stain Removal Stick

Braided Elastic Laundry Line means you don't have to pack clothes pins because the elastic holds the clothes securely.

Concentrated Travel Soap It works in cold water, hot water, salt water, etc. A traveler once told me he wears all his dirty clothes right into the shower and starts with his head: washes his hair, his clothes, body, down to his socks. (Most women are horrified at the thought of this but know men who would do it!). This type of soap usually works great for removing chlorine from swimsuits. (FYI: Certain destinations require biodegradable soap, so know before you go.)

A Sink Stopper to plug a drain. Many hotels do not provide these because they'd prefer you to send your laundry out to be cleaned. Travel with a multi-purpose, 5 inch diameter, thin, rubber disk. It's also useful for opening jars, removing lint from clothing and as a bath plug.

A Travel Towel made out of Micro Fiber. Quick drying micro fiber absorbs water quickly. Roll up your washed items in it to absorb the water and your clothes will dry faster. The large size is useful as you can use it as a cover-up for your swimsuit, a beach towel and even as a blanket on the plane.

Inflatable Hangers made of durable vinyl inflate to allow your drip dry blouses, bathing suits, and sweaters to dry without hanger creases. Also provides you with extra hangers. They can be used also at home for fine lingerie. And you won't get rust from scary old hotel hangers on your nice clean clothes.

A Stain Removal Stick will save the day. Always keep one in your laundry kit for quick spot removal.

A Zip-Clean Travel Washing Machine really works! When it comes to doing laundry in the sink, do you ever wonder how clean the sink really is? Use a gallon size Ziploc® bag as a mini-washing machine. Just put in your socks, soap and water and agitate or knead it for awhile. Repeat with clean water for the "rinse-cycle." Pack pre-measured travel soap in snack-sized bags and combine all your laundry items: laundry line, sink stopper, inflatable hangers, etc. inside a gallon size bag so you always have everything organized.

More Laundry Secrets

- Some old-style sinks are funneled too deep for the disc sink-stopper to work efficiently. For these, you can use a small heavy children's rubber ball (2"). This stops up any size drain and you also have something to play with along your travels.

- Ice cubes work great on grease spills on clothing while dining out if nothing else is available. The stain won't set in.

- Sample sizes of dishwashing liquid, mailed as promotions, are great for getting grease out of clothes, and they are unbreakable (put in plastic bag to be safe).

- Don't forget to take a small packet of cold water soap just in case you can't find hot water.

- Take along a small spray bottle. When you have a wrinkle in cottons, linen or any washable item, simply fill the bottle with tap water and spray the wrinkles. In a short time the wrinkles will disappear.

- Use mesh laundry bags for packing similar items together making them easier to find. For example, underwear, t-shirts and especially small items like socks.

- Compression bags work great for dirty laundry and for damp work out clothes that don't have time to dry before you pack them.

- Be sure to pack some dryer sheets in case you find a dryer on your travels.

- Think twice about traveling in jeans. If you need to wash them, they'll take a very long time to dry.

- 12 -
Tips for Plane Trips

Of the many different forms of transportation, plane travel can be one of the most stressful if you're not prepared. The key to reducing stress is to arrive at the airport with plenty of time to spare. You'll need time to check your bags and get through security checkpoints as well as time for last minute things like making phone calls and using the facilities.

It's recommended that you arrive at least 90 minutes prior to domestic flights and 2-1/2 hours for International flights (check with your airline).

To help ensure a smooth trip, it's important to plan ahead and have certain essentials with you to make the trip more enjoyable. The following suggestions will help you maximize your time in the airport, arrive rested and ready to hit the ground running after any flight.

Tips

- If you have a cold or any other physical problem that you are concerned about, be sure to consult your physician before any flight. Cabin pressure changes can be painful if you're congested.

- At the ticket counter, always have the ticket agent confirm your return flights, as well as reserve your seat if you don't already have one.

- To minimize delays, opt for the first flight of the day.

- Check your baggage claim tickets immediately after they are stapled into your ticket jacket and/or attached to your luggage. Make sure they match and that you have all of them. Everyone makes mistakes, and it's easier to catch them right away.

- Before leaving home for the airport, call to find out if your flight is on-time. Do so likewise when picking someone up at the airport. Weather conditions often cause delays, and you shouldn't spend needless time (and money for parking) waiting for other's arrival.

When picking someone up at the airport, arrange to meet them outside the *departure* area (the opposite of what you would normally do). There isn't usually a huge crush of cars all vying for the curb as there is at the *arrival* area.

- Upon arrival at the airport, check the monitors immediately to see if your flight is on time and from which gate it departs.

- Enjoy your time at the airport. Use it to check-out the different shops, which may include bookstores, card stores, and various specialty boutiques. Just remember, they are usually expensive.

- In large airports, where you have to change terminals for your next flight, ask the flight attendant how to get to your next departure gate. You may need to take a tram, sky train or walk long distances.

- If your checked luggage arrives damaged, report it promptly to an airline representative before you leave the airport.

 One of my favorite tips is: Fly the day before you need to be at your destination. This helps alleviate stress in case you encounter weather or mechanical delays along the way. This will also allow delayed luggage time to catch up with you. Your best bet is to arrive at your destination rested and relaxed, so you can start your trip immediately, or at least with a small amount of rest time.

Tips to Help Reduce Jet Lag

For many travelers, the real turbulence begins after a flight. Crossing time zones disrupts your body clock and can lead to sleepy days, sleepless nights, and more.

To help prevent jet lag, get plenty of sleep before your trip and drink water on the plane, not alcohol. The dry air in airplanes causes dehydration and drinking plenty of non-alcoholic fluids helps counter this. (However, when I told my father this tip, his reply was, "Why on earth would I fly if I can't have a drink?") As with all the tips in this book, some will work for you, some won't.

A few other suggestions

- Limit your intake of caffeine and salt, eat bland foods a few days before the trip, and don't eat spicy foods en-route.

- Adjust your sleeping habits before leaving home. Check the time zone to which you're headed and go to sleep an hour earlier than usual (or later, depending on which direction). Allow your body to adjust.

- Once you're on the plane, change your watch to

your destination time zone. I don't know if it's all psychological, but it works for me.

- Upon arrival, take a long warm shower. More than a few travelers have suggested this tip. They say it helps restore some hydration to your body (and it helps wake you up).

- Homeopathic remedies are also available, check travel stores and catalogs.

Food In the Air

- Isn't it funny, for years we all joked about airline food and now we miss it. Call your airline to see if there will be a meal offered (and whether it's complimentary) and ask if you can order a special meal in advance. Hey, stranger things have happened!

- Always travel with food. Ramen noodles and instant soup can be mixed with a cup of hot water to make an instant meal on the plane. Dried cranberries, nuts and nutrition bars are also good.

- Place some extra food or breakfast bars in the outer pocket of your carry-on just in case you become stranded in an airport. Sometimes, airports close down early.

- Pack fiber bars - for the obvious reason!

Comfort En-Route

- Travel with your own "Plane Comfort Pocket" which includes a blanket, eye shades, inflatable pillow and ear plugs all packed in one bag. See AM FAVE on page 81.

- An inflatable neck pillow is perfect to save your neck from kinks. A lumbar pillow used at the small of your back greatly relieves tired shoulders. I always travel with my own neck and lumbar pillow in my carry-on bag.

- Here's a unique plane pillow idea: Bring an inflatable beach ball. When you get on the plane and are ready for a head rest, blow the ball half way up or until comfortable. You can have fun with it when you get off the plane.

- Sleeping is easier when you block out light and sound. Pack eye-shades and ear-plugs for help sleeping while flying.

- If you find it difficult to sleep on planes due to the noise, try noise canceling headphones.

- On long flights (especially international flights), wear casual clothing and change in the restroom before claiming your baggage. The key here is to be comfortable.

- Pack a pair of socks in your carry-on (in case you're not wearing any) to keep your toes warm. Airplane temperatures change constantly.

- After your flight reaches cruising altitude, remove your shoes and scrunch your toes around — it helps!

- Some travelers wear compression socks to help with circulation while traveling. These socks can help reduce swelling and help prevent blood clots. Ask your doctor for a recommendation.

- To help circulation, prop your feet on your carry-on bag. (Of course make sure that you don't have any breakables near the surface).

- For contact lens wearers: Carry a travel-sized bottle of saline solution in your carry-on. The air on planes can dry them out. Be sure to bring your spare glasses and a lens case with you in your carry-on. You don't want to be without these items in the event your checked luggage is lost.

- Keep a small spray bottle of water in your carry-on to keep your face and arms moisturized at high altitudes. Also take a travel-sized bottle of lotion and eye drops.

- Many find the best solution to keep their ears clear while flying is to chew gum. Use it on both the ascent and descent. Or try a sip of water from your water bottle. It helps you stay hydrated in a dry environment, as well.

- Many travelers recommend special ear-plugs specifically designed to relieve ear pressure during take off and landing. Inquire at travel and luggage stores.

Airplane Seating

- Reasons couples may wish to occupy opposite aisle seats are: (1) to avoid climbing over passengers on the way to the rest room, (2) there is a higher probability of having a vacant seat since the center seat is usually always the last one assigned, and (3) guaranteed use of at least one arm rest!

- Request an emergency exit row for more leg room. Be sure you are capable of assisting in an emergency and can fit the criteria for this row. Some airlines charge extra for these seats and some of these seats do not recline. (Be sure to ask when you book).

- A window seat is best for sleeping since no one will crawl over you to get to the restroom or the overhead compartment.

- An aisle seat is best for stretching your legs and for those who may need to frequent the facilities.

- Request a bulkhead seat when you are traveling with children, a wheelchair or cane. (Keep in mind that you may be sitting beside people with special needs and may be interrupted often.) The drawback is there is nowhere to stow your bag in front of you during take off and landing so you'll have to retrieve it once the plane reaches cruising altitude.

- Avoid seats across from or near restrooms.

- Ask the flight attendant if the plane is fully booked. If not, you may be able to make yourself more comfortable by moving to another area of the plane and stretch out.

More Tips for Plane Trips

- Take your seat immediately when boarding starts. This way, you are almost always guaranteed your seat in case of over-booking, as you will already be sitting in it.

- Always leave your shoes on until the aircraft has reached cruising altitude- just in case you have to evacuate the aircraft in an emergency.

- If you like reading on flights, bring a book light. Sometimes the plane light at your seat may not work. Or use your travel flashlight.

"Never a ship sails out of the bay, but carries my heart as a stowaway."

Roselle Mercier Montgomery

- 13 -
Cruising Tips

Cruising is one of the most popular vacation choices offered to travelers. Although cruises have been around for years, there are now many more lines and itineraries to choose from. These days, it seems like everyone is cruising.

The benefit of a cruise vacation is that almost every detail of your trip is taken care of for you. Be familiar with your cruise line's brochure and know exactly what is and what is not included in the price, which varies greatly from line to line. For example, some cruise lines include your shore excursions in the total cruise fare, but most do not. This can make a huge difference in price if you intend to take advantage of the ship's tour program. There are also some wonderful enhancement programs available on most cruise lines which can "enhance" your experience on board. Be sure to check in advance.

Luggage tips

One of the best things about cruising is you only have to unpack once! The downside is, since you don't have to lug your stuff around for 2 weeks, travelers tend to pack too much for cruise vacations. Hopefully, the following tips will help you pack less stuff more efficiently for your cruise.

While the majority of cruise lines do not have specific

baggage allowances, you have to consider how you're getting to the port. If you're driving to the port, there's no problem. However, airlines do have baggage allowances, so it is recommended that you check with the airline on which you're traveling to see what those allowances are. And, keep in mind that once at your destination, transfer vehicles may have baggage restrictions.

Remember that checked baggage might not be accessible at all times. A solution to this problem is the 16" rolling tote. This bag plus a small tote bag allows you to carry-on everything you'll need for the first 1-2 days of your cruise, including a change of clothes for the first evening upon embarkation. The wheels make it a breeze to carry heavy items such as medicines, cameras, binoculars, etc. through long cruise ship terminals and up gangways. See page 29 for more information on rolling tote bags.

Tips

- Remember to bring your travel and health insurance information with you and have it handy at all times.

- Double check that your identification and travel tickets are in your personal carry-on bag and available at all times.

- As with any type of travel, never pack anything of value in your checked luggage.

- When you pack your cruise carry-on bag, try packing everything you will need for the first three days in this bag. With the chance of lost or delayed luggage, especially if you arrive at your destination the same day you set sail, you may sail without your checked bags.

- In addition to a 16" rolling tote and a small tote bag, most cruisers should be able to pack enough clothing into a 24" rolling suitcase for a 1-2 week cruise (See Cruise Wardrobe Planner page 108). Remember, there will be times when you will need to handle your luggage on your own and you want to be able to stack and roll easily. Consider expandable luggage since you know you're going to do some shopping!!

- Always be sure to place an ID tag on your bag. Most cruise lines will give you special baggage tags with your cruise documentation and instructions on how, when and where to place them on your bags before you leave home.

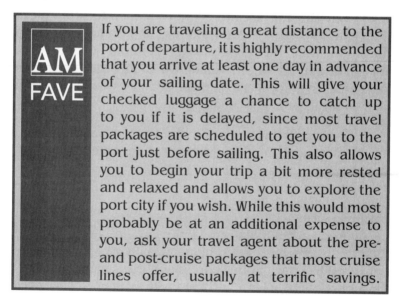

If you are traveling a great distance to the port of departure, it is highly recommended that you arrive at least one day in advance of your sailing date. This will give your checked luggage a chance to catch up to you if it is delayed, since most travel packages are scheduled to get you to the port just before sailing. This also allows you to begin your trip a bit more rested and relaxed and allows you to explore the port city if you wish. While this would most probably be at an additional expense to you, ask your travel agent about the pre- and post-cruise packages that most cruise lines offer, usually at terrific savings.

- Another option for your luggage is to forward it to the ship before your cruise or forward it home after the cruise. Inquire with your travel agent.

Organizing Your Cruise Wardrobe

The right clothing can make or break your cruise. First and foremost, dress for comfort. Daily life aboard ship and in ports of call is laid-back and casual. Wear whatever makes you feel most comfortable: sportswear, shorts, sundresses, slacks, and so on. Warmer climates call for clothing made of lightweight, breathable fabrics. For cooler climates, pack casual clothes that layer easily. A raincoat, waterproof hat and gloves, and an umbrella might be in order. And remember, certain destinations may require particular attention to clothing. For example, certain churches, or other places of worship, may not allow tank tops or short pants.

Don't forget your swimsuit — most cruise ships have pools, saunas and hot tubs. You may wish to bring more than one swimsuit if you'll be spending a lot of time in the water. Remember to wear shoes and a cover-up over your bathing suit when walking through the interior of the ship. If you'd like to jog on deck or work-out in the fitness center, bring workout gear.

Footwear should include comfortable walking shoes for visits ashore and sandals or rubber-soled shoes for strolling on deck.

Evening Dress

Evening dress usually falls into two categories: Smart Casual and Formal. Each night, a daily program will be delivered to your cabin announcing the suggested dress for the following evening. Check with your travel agent or refer to your cruise brochure.

Smart Casual

Smart Casual is comfortable relaxed clothing. Tank tops and shorts are not usually allowed in the restaurants or public areas during evening hours. Some cruise lines allow jeans in the restaurants for dinner, but not all. Check in advance.

Formal

There are usually one or two formal nights per week on most cruises. For formal evenings, women usually wear cocktail dresses or skirt/pants with a dressy top. Men usually wear a suit and tie or tuxedo.

Ask your travel agent to find-out specifically how many casual and formal nights your cruise will have. This varies from line to line and itinerary. Make a list of what clothes you plan to wear to cut-down on over-packing.

Also, ask your travel agent for suggestions if you need additional advice or ask him/her to refer you to a client that has just returned from the cruise line on which you are sailing. First-hand knowledge is invaluable.

Use the "Cruise Wardrobe Planner" on the following page to help you organize your wardrobe.

Wardrobe Planning Tips

- Most importantly, take into consideration the type of cruising that you will be doing. Obviously, a weekend cruise is more casual than a world cruise.

- Remember that black is always formal (or navy blue). You can dress-up an outfit many different ways with a minimal amount of accessories when you wear black. This saves purchasing additional clothes.

Pack It Up—Cruise Wardrobe Planner

	Port	Daytime Outfit	Evening Outfit	*	Special Events & Activities
Day 1					
Day 2					
Day 3					
Day 4					
Day 5					
Day 6					
Day 7					

*Use this column to indicate ship's suggested evening dress   C- Casual   F-Formal

©Pack It Up

- Many people choose cruising because they enjoy "dressing" for dinner and having the opportunity to wear fine jewelry. This seems to work well for most people, but remember, you must get to the ship via airplanes, buses, etc., and that jewelry should be kept in a safe when you're not wearing it. This can be very time consuming and worrisome, so it is suggested that you carefully weigh the pros and cons of bringing valuables on your cruise.

- Many cruises offer "Theme Nights" and your travel agent will supply you with a list of those in advance. Ask your friends and relatives if they have an item of clothing you can borrow before you purchase something that you probably won't wear again.

- The potential expense of a cruise wardrobe is the formal attire. Women passengers wear almost anything from nice pants to sequin gowns. Unless a gentleman enjoys wearing a tuxedo, it's not necessary to bring one. A dark suit with tie works fine. Usually the longer the cruise the fancier the dress.

- For formal night, a woman would feel quite acceptable in a medium-to-long dress, or a skirt with a fancy top/blouse. A black skirt works well, as you can change several different tops and scarves to dress it up or down. A pair of nice black pants with a variety of blouses and low black heels can turn simpler clothes into a variety of looks.

- Longer faux pearl necklaces can be more versatile and shortened with a pearl clip for a different look. Matching earrings with a bit of rhinestone look very elegant.

- Rhinestone necklaces and bracelets are fun to

wear but expensive to buy. Ask someone who just returned from a cruise if they might have some you could borrow, or check second-hand stores for great savings.

- Don't forget an evening clutch bag or one with a strap. Again, stay with a basic color scheme and check department or vintage clothing stores for specials. A money saving tip: convert your simple black travel purse to a fancy evening bag by simply pinning a rhinestone pin to the outside. It really dresses it up! Tuck the straps to the inside of the bag and you have a nice clutch.

- When packing your luggage, pack your jewelry inside your evening bag so you know where it is. Never pack valuable jewelry.

- If you are on a clothing budget, ask friends and family to lend you some fancy things they may not be using. Check into formal wear rentals for women as well as men. Some cruise lines offer a rental service.

- Elastic-waisted clothing is essential for those who enjoy eating (and isn't that one of the main attractions of a cruise)? Here's a tip: Use a heavy duty rubber band if your pants are too tight and loop it through the button and buttonhole. It's said that the salt air shrinks your clothes when you're at sea. Either way, be comfortable!

General Cruising Tips

- Pack an outfit that doubles as exercise wear. Many passengers discover great programs onboard designed for all levels of fitness and wish they had brought clothing in which to exercise. It's a great way to meet friends and also justify that second helping of chocolate volcano!

- If you are a serious exercise enthusiast, check into different cruise lines. Most offer fantastic exercise programs and state of-the-art gym equipment. On some lines, entire theme cruises are planned around the exercise program. Be sure to confirm that the ship you choose has a fitness director onboard.

- Ships' activities are a great way to meet new friends. All lines' activities vary, so ask your travel agent if he/she has a recent copy of the daily activities program from the ship you are looking into. Culinary, computer and crafts classes are often available.

- For solo-travelers, cruises are a great way to meet new people. Many cruises offer activities designed specifically for people traveling on their own.

- If you're not sure of your way around the ship and did not receive a map upon embarkation, ask the front office for one.

- Bring a bathing cap (which can double as a shower cap in a pinch!). Many cruise ship swimming pools are salt water, which can be damaging to your hair if it's chemically treated or very dry. Take extra conditioner along for your hair just in case.

- A pashmina (wrap) is a must if you tend to chill easily. Whether for a nice stroll out on deck under the stars or for the air-conditioned lounges, you'll be glad you brought it. Black is a good color choice as it can be used on formal nights as well (and won't show dirt as easily as white).

- A sarong makes a handy cover-up for the pool or beach. It's easy to tie and wear while sitting at the counter for a refreshing drink, or as a throw when you've had too much sun. Please see page 161 for ideas on how to tie your Sarong.

- A packable straw hat is perfect for a cruise, rolls to pack and won't fray or crack.

- Always pack comfortable shoes when traveling but especially on a ship that is constantly moving. Take comfortable walking shoes for visits ashore and sandals or rubber soled shoes for strolling on deck. Low heels are much more practical for evening wear.

- If you are traveling with children or grandchildren, make sure that the ship you're on caters to them. There are certain lines that specialize in children's programs with entire daily schedules printed just for them. Generally, the peak cruising times for children are major holidays, so if you prefer the company of adults only, choose your schedule accordingly.

- Since the sun's rays are much stronger at sea than on land, screening-out the sun's harmful rays is important. Wear extra sunscreen and a hat. A visor is helpful if you like to read in the sun. Don't forget the effects of sun reflected off water if you are poolside or at the beach. The same effect exists with snow on the colder itineraries such as Alaska. And don't overlook protection for your lips! Select a lip balm that includes a sunscreen to help combat the effects of the wind, sun and salt air.

- Instead of taking your old paperback home, suggest a paperback exchange, if there isn't one already setup by the staff. This is a great way to meet someone and trade your old book for a new one for the trip home.

 Pack books that you haven't had time to read yet. If you forgot one, most ships have libraries. A tip on ships' libraries: check out the book selection as soon as you have a chance. Passengers tend to linger over books they've borrowed, and the selection is greatly reduced after the first few days at sea.

- If you do forget something, remember that the ship's shops usually carry items that you need. In addition, check their daily specials, as many a great buy has been made when you take into account that the majority of these shops are duty-free. Even on cruises with ideal shopping destinations, remember the ship's shops have competitive prices.

- If you wear panty-hose, bring a few pairs with you. This is one article of clothing that varies greatly from one brand to another, especially the size.

- Most cruise ship cabins are equipped with standard 110 AC and 220 AC outlets and provide hair dryers. Guests with pre or post-cruise hotel packages may want to bring converters and/or adapters for their hotel stay.

- Give yourself permission to take a night off and just relax! Why not use the time to do some laundry while you're finishing up that book you've been too busy to read? Some large cruise ships have laundry rooms with coin operated washers and dryers and even irons and ironing boards. This works especially well for 10 day or longer cruises, as you can pack less clothes.

 Take a postcard of your ship with you ashore. This way you have a picture to show cab drivers, etc. where you need to return in case of a language barrier.

Communication At Sea

When you're on vacation, it's always reassuring to leave the telephone number of your destination with family, friends and work associates.

Telephone: Direct ship-to-shore telephones are provided in most guest staterooms. Check with your Travel Agent or cruise brochure. Most cruise lines provide "communications cards" when you book your cruise or receive your tickets. Distribute these to friends and relatives so they will know how to contact you in case of an emergency back home or just to say hello. Cards also enable you to send/receive faxes.

Mobile Phones: You may also be able to make and receive calls on your own cell phone while at sea so take it with you. Depending on your cellular provider, you might be able to send and receive text messages. Rates are similar to international roaming rates, set by each home carrier and usually appear as roaming charges on your regular bill. Check before leaving home with your carrier for all possible charges.

E-mail and Internet: On almost all cruise ships, you can send and receive e-mail from the ship's computer workstations or wirelessly on your laptop. Ship common areas have "hot spots" for personal laptops. Be sure to bring your password and e-mail addresses with you.

VOIP: The use of service requires compatible cell phones/PDA's/laptops with a cellular provider that has a roaming agreement with the cruise line. Check in advance if available and cost involved since no one likes expensive surprises.

TV: Most ships provide in-cabin televisions for viewing news, movies and onboard features. Reception varies depending on your itinerary.

Newspapers: The ship usually prints a bulletin of the day's news happening around the world. After ports of call, check the ship's library for newspapers that might have been brought aboard for guests.

Money Matters

Once you're checked-in, you will receive a ship identification card. This ship ID card serves as your identification for security procedures when embarking and disembarking the ship, and for making purchases onboard. Ordinarily, it doubles as your access card to your cabin. Tip: In some situations you may also have to show a valid government picture ID whenever getting on/off the ship in addition to your ship's ID. Confirm onboard your ship.

The majority of cruise lines have a "cashless" policy for all purchases made onboard. You simply show your ship's ID and the charge is placed on your account. You may choose to add a gratuity on food and drink, if it has not been added automatically. Always check your bill.

For ease in settling your account, cruise lines encourage you to leave an imprint of your credit card prior or during embarkation. Your itemized bill will be sent to your cabin directly for your approval, usually the day before you disembark. This eliminates standing in line on the last day. Most cruise lines do not have ATM machines onboard and do not accept personal checks.

Selecting a Cabin

Your travel agent is the most important source of information for all your travel needs. But you must provide some information about yourself so he/she can find the cabin best suited to your needs.

Here are some suggestions:

- If you tend to get seasick or think you might, a mid-ships cabin would be a good idea. To be away from the pitching and rolling of the topside and lower decks, mid-ship will be the most stable.

- Do you want/need a verandah or suite? Check the prices in the different categories. If you don't plan on spending much time in your cabin, a verandah maybe an added expense that you may not need.

- An inside cabin will cost less, however, they can be small and obviously dark without access to natural light.

- Are you a light sleeper? Check what's above your cabin, i.e. lounges, dining rooms, etc. which might keep you awake.

- If you prefer a queen or king size bed, make sure that the ship you have chosen can accommodate your request. Some of the older ships are furnished with twin beds only.

- If you use a wheelchair, make sure that your cabin and bathroom are accessible. And make sure there is an elevator in the vicinity. Read the diagram in the brochure to find out about the layout of the ship and ask your travel agent's advice, too.

Dining Tips

These days, cruise ships offer many options for dining. Depending on the ship, these options include: a) elegant dining with assigned seating at the same scheduled time and with the same people, b) flexible dining where you still enjoy the main dining restaurant, however, you are not tied down to a scheduled time and c) casual dining which allows you to choose the venue that suits you best from cafes to pizzeria's.

- If you prefer set dining arrangements, you usually have a choice of two sittings - generally called "early" and "late." The early-sitting usually begins at 6 p.m. and the late around 8 p.m. Since the evenings' entertainment usually follows your dinner, second-sitting is generally for the younger or more late-night crowd, which enjoys a show beginning after 10 p.m. The first-sitting show usually begins around 8 p.m.

- If you do have a preference on sitting times, be sure to request it from your travel agent. Remember, though, that while the cruise line will try to accommodate your request, it may not always be possible to do so.

- Also, request to sit with any specific friends with whom you are traveling. Table sizes run anywhere from an intimate table for two to a large table for eight. Many passengers prefer a large table, figuring that out of eight people there will be interesting conversationalists.

- If you have received your seating arrangements and

they are not what you requested, contact the Maitre d' as soon as possible (or the person in charge of the sitting assignments). For some passengers, this is the most important part of their cruise. Remember, a smile and a polite handshake go a long distance to remedy a situation.

- And it's nice to know that you can choose a variety of the above mentioned options for dining. For example, on formal night, you might prefer to dine in the dining room. Upon returning to the ship late in the day, you might prefer a more casual dinner in the café instead of rushing into the shower and the formality of the dining room.

- If you have special dietary requirements, request these when booking your cruise. Make sure the ship you're cruising on can accommodate your requirements. Remember that this is an extra service, so your patience and understanding go a long way during the first few meals with a new waiter.

- Many large cruise ships have specialty restaurants which require reservations. Ask your travel agent if advanced reservations are accepted as they usually fill up quickly. Note: There is usually an additional cost to dine in these restaurants.

Seasickness

With today's modern technology and stabilizers, there is little chance of seasickness among passengers. But, if you are susceptible to motion sickness, be sure to check with your physician before leaving home. There are many different products on the market to help, though these may have different side effects for different people.

- Motion bands, a non-medicinal aid for seasickness

(and most motion sickness), is a favorite among passengers. These are elasticized wrist bands that apply slight pressure on the acupressure point near each wrist that controls nausea.

● For severe cases of seasickness, there are other options, like a patch or injection, available on most ships from the physician. Consult your doctor at home and onboard before making any decisions.

● A few suggestions to help queasy stomachs: Dry foods, such as bread, breadsticks or crackers, help to settle the uneasy feeling experienced in rough seas. Also limit liquids.

Tips on Tipping

Tipping varies greatly from ship to ship, depending on which service was performed and how.

Most cruise lines add a Hotel Service Charge automatically to your shipboard account, which covers dining room wait staff and cabin stewards. If their service exceeds or fails to meet your expectations, you are free to adjust this amount at the end of the cruise.

The amount varies, however it's generally $12 per day, per person.

A 15% service charge is generally added automatically to bar charges and dining room wine purchases. A note: If you receive a complimentary bottle of wine, it is customary to tip the wine steward for this service just as if you had purchased the wine yourself. Also, tipping of the Maitre d' and the head waiter for any special meals or assistance is customarily $10-$20 at the end of the cruise.

In terminals, airports, ports of calls and on-shore excursions, you should extend gratuities consistent with customary local practices.

More Tips

- At the end of the cruise, a disembarkation talk for all passengers is held. It is suggested that one member of each party or family attends because information is given regarding disembarkation procedures, customs, luggage tags, airline connections and so on. This will insure that you will have a pleasant, stress-free ending to your cruise.

- On the last night of your cruise, you will need to place your luggage, with the provided luggage tags, outside your cabin before you retire. You will find ship-specific information onboard. Make sure you have clothes and toiletries with you for your travel day. Once again, the rolling tote to the rescue!

- Place a luggage ID tag inside your luggage, as well as on the outside.

- Be sure to keep together your personal identification, airline tickets, customs forms, medications, and other important items along with the clothes and shoes you intend to wear the next day during your trip home. Place them in your carry-on bag or on your person so you can access them easily.

Pack a Sense of Humor

Years ago, on an Alaskan cruise, I was standing on a small dock with about 35 passengers, waiting for our tender to pick us up and take us to our ship. Near me were two wonderful ladies: 92 year old Mrs. Philpott and 89 year old Mrs. Marler. Before our tender came, a fishing boat pulled up and bumped the side of the dock causing most of us to lose our balance. There was no railing around the dock, and before we knew what was happening, Mrs. Philpott grabbed a hold of Mrs. Marler to steady her, and they both went over the side into 30 degree water. The first thing Mrs. Philpott said when we fished her out was, "I'll have to have my hair redone!"

The best part of the story happened two days later when they both came to the Masquerade party dressed as icebergs!

As they walked into the lounge, I told them how inspirational they were and what a wonderful sense of humor they both had. Mrs. Philpott took my hand, looked me right in the eye and said, "You know Anne, by the time you're 92 years old, you will realize, it's your sense of humor that keeps you going."

121

Always pack your sense of humor.

Anne McAlpin

- 14 -
Car Tips for Road Trips

Whether you're packing a car, a mini-van or an RV, there are a few basic principles to keep in mind. (1) Keep the front seat area as the command center — no distractions. (2) When packing the car, place the heaviest items on the bottom and don't pack higher than the seat back so items don't shift in a sudden stop. (3) Pack the most important items you'll need on your trip last, so they're the easiest to find!

Front Seat Area

- Keep your cell phone in the front seat area and use a hands free adapter for safety. Better yet, have someone traveling with you make the call.

- Keep your travel atlas with-in easy reach: In the pocket of the door.

 Instead of struggling with a huge a map, cut out the area you'll be traveling through, use a highlighter to outline the route and place it inside a plastic sleeve for quick reference.

- Pack your car's emergency kit and first aid kit under your seats for easy access.

- Clean out your glove compartment and replace only what you need. Keep a flashlight handy for emergencies or just to read a map. Also keep tissues, wet-ones and sunglasses close at hand.

- Keep a compass in your glove compartment for finding your way in unfamiliar areas. This has saved many marriages.

Middle Seats

- A backseat organizer is perfect for keeping items from rolling around on the floor of your car. These hook over the headrest and have multiple pockets for such items as: umbrellas, magazines, paper towels, water bottles, etc. You can pack one for kids with snacks and make it an activity center filled with things to do while in the car.

- Use every bit of space: A 12 pack of soda/beverages fits under the middle seat of a van.

- Freeze a few water bottles before you leave home. You'll have very cold water to drink as it starts melting. Better to fill only half the bottle as the water may expand to cause cracks in the bottle. Also, if you only freeze half the bottle, you won't have to wait 3 hours to get the first few sips out.

Rear Section of Car

- If your car has a lift-up compartment in the back, like a tire-well, it's perfect for packing breakables, gifts and items that might get crushed (like a bottle of wine). Line it first with a blanket.

- Always conceal valuables in your trunk or under cover for protection.

- Pack the heaviest items in your car first, on the bottom. Pack the perimeter with soft, squishable unbreakable items to help cushion items in the middle.

- Cardboard six packs markets use for wine purchases are very helpful. They fold flat and when needed, keep new purchases from rolling around in boxes and totes.

- Collapsible crates (available for about $5 at home improvement stores) are great for car travel. Open and stack when needed, collapse and save space when not.

 Pack a different colored bag per person. Brightly-colored tote bags help identify what's organized where. Squish, stuff and stack.

- Pack coolers so they are easily accessible.

- Pack all your sun/beach items together in one tote bag: Sunscreen, sunglasses, swimsuit, hat, towel, etc. so you can hit the beach running.

Car Tips for Kid Trips

- Place an upside-down cardboard box between the kids in the middle or backseat. This serves two purposes: (1) As a writing surface, (2) keeps kids separated.

- Before you spend money at a toy store, check out your kitchen: A 9"x13" covered tin cake pan makes a great "lap desk" for kids in the car. Pack all their colored pencils, paper, crafts inside and they have a flat surface to write on the top.

Use cookie sheets as drawing surfaces for your children. Cut a piece of non skid shelf liner to fit the inside and use the ones with the lip on the edge to help keep pens from sliding off. You can find used ones at thrift stores or garage sales.

- Keep an empty baby wipes container (the square, pop-up kind) filled with used plastic grocery sacks in your car. On trips, long or short, you always have a bag handy for trash, dirty kids clothes, or wet swim items. Keep it under the seat.

- Office supply stores have a great variety of plastic containers that teenagers like. Packed with some fun gel pens, paper and note pads, this makes a nice gift to give them before you go and keeps them busy en-route.

- Keep a backpack fully stocked within arms reach for each child.

- Pack pillows and blankets for everyone for travel and use at your destination.

- Here's an easy solution to the age-old question of who gets the front seat, window, etc. (if you have children who are born on odd/even days). On odd numbered days, the child with the odd numbered birthday would have the first choice and on the even numbered day, etc.

- A blank US map for each child can be fun to color-in as license plates from different states are spotted. Download maps free from the internet.

- Pack a jump rope in your backseat organizer so kids can burn off some energy when you reach the rest area.

- A Frisbee is a must for car travel with kids. They are inexpensive, fun to play with at rest stops and can be used as plates in a pinch.

- Keep a pair of flip flops for each child in the back seat pocket for quick rest stops so they don't have to put their shoes on.

- Plan your picnics at playgrounds so there's something fun and new for the kids to do while you relax and have something to eat.

- Pack a mesh drawstring bag for wet jackets, clothing or towels. The open mesh allows air to circulate so you won't end up with mildewy items.

- Keep some extra kitchen towels in the car for use if your coffee spills or to catch crumbs when eating in the car. With a splash of water, they can be used to do a quick clean up, too.

- Pack lots of garbage bags for all types of uses.

"On a long journey, even a straw
weighs heavy."

Spanish proverb

- 15 -
Great Ideas!

Over the years, I have picked-up numerous travel and packing tips from the travelers that I have met along my journeys. From solo travelers to cruise passengers to tour members, they've passed-on the following hints and swear to their effectiveness in making their trip just a little bit easier. Even the most seasoned traveler should be able to pick up a few new travel tips from among these:

- Tip for golfers: Buy a cheap hockey stick and saw off the blade. Cut the remaining shaft to 46" (make sure the length is approx. 1" longer than your driver or 3 wood). Insert in golf bag. If your bag is dropped by the airlines the hockey stick will take the force of the drop and you will not have a bent or broken shaft.

- For those travelers who enjoy making things with their hands, crocheting is a great way to kill time in airports, on long flights, train and bus rides. Take a crochet hook along and using locally bought yarn along the way, create something that will remind you of your trip once you get home.

- Here's a great tip for those who like to travel extremely light. When you arrive in a new country, go to a backpacker's hostel and see who is ready to get rid of some gear... and buy it used. Conversely, when you're ready to leave, do the same.

- When traveling over the holidays, ship your gifts in advance. No need to worry about delayed luggage and missing presents.

- To secure your buttons, put a drop of fabric glue on each button prior to departure (available at fabric stores). It seals your buttons.

- Pack travel binoculars (or a monocular) for walking tours, concerts, wildlife, etc. These fit into your pocket and most come with a case which includes a loop to attach on your belt.

- Take a small compass. It's great for navigating a new city in a rental car. Clip it on your bag so it's handy to find your direction when reading a map. Solves the problem of knowing which way is North when you exit a museum or the subway.

- Take your portable dash GPS from your car along. No need to pay rental fees or figure out a new piece of technology.

- A lot of travelers enjoy a drink before dinner or a nightcap, but room service can be expensive (or non existent at some destinations). Buy an 8oz (or 16 oz!) plastic bottle and fill with your favorite drink (vodka, gin, bourbon). Pack inside a plastic bag and slip inside your shoes in your checked-in luggage.

- Wrap duct tape a few times around a mailing tube. This will provide you with a lot of duct tape if you need it and you'll have a tube for bringing home new art purchased along the way.

- Another use for duct tape while traveling: If the curtains of your hotel don't quite close all the way, you can tape them shut.

- For safety when sightseeing: Wear a waist pack positioned in the front so when you stop to take photos, you don't have to set your purse on the ground. Your camera and film are easily accessible.

- A very useful travel essential is a 3 foot retractable corded cable with a combination lock. It allows you to lock a group of luggage together when you go into a restaurant or secure your bags to the metal rack in a train compartment. It can also be used as a bike lock, ski lock, etc. Approx. $15

- Since some socks take forever to dry, try traveling with a pair or two of hiking sock liners. These help prevent blisters and drip dry quickly.

- Take an emergency blanket and a $1 rain poncho. They both work great as ground cover for a picnic, table cloth, luggage cover, coat, etc.

- Save clean napkins from the breakfast table for your day's journey. They can provide a quick clean up.

- Test your camera before your vacation to ensure that it is still functioning. This is important for both new and old cameras alike.

Can't seem to save enough money for your dream vacation? Make a "dream jar" by decorating a coffee can (or any container) with magazine photos of your dream destination. Put it in the kitchen and every time you decide to eat in instead of dining out, put the extra money you've saved into your "dream" vacation fund.

- Check batteries in your travel flashlight and remove them when not in use. For emergencies, place the flashlight near your bed when going to sleep.

- Don't forget to take extra batteries for everything. They may be impossible to find, and also expensive, in certain countries. You don't want to waste precious sightseeing time in a frustrating search. This includes hearing aid batteries.

- Always travel with safety pins. If a button pops off, fix it using a safety pin.

- Pack a small, foam-gripped pen on an 18 inch retractable cord that clips to your belt loop, or bag strap. It is small and conveniently accessible.

- Another use for a hotel shower cap: It works great for keeping your saddle dry on your bike from rain and dew. The elastic fits snuggly around it and will keep it from blowing off.

- If you enjoy visiting wineries on your travels, pack a corkscrew. Sampling your new discoveries in your hotel room that night can be fun. For tips on packing wine, check out **www.packitup.com**.

- Dryer sheets or air fresheners can be very useful while traveling: Freshen up a hotel room, drawer, closet, rental car, shoes, etc.

More great AM travel tips

- Secure the shoulder strap of your carry-on around your foot or chair leg when seated. This acts as an anchor if the bag is grabbed.

- Copy jokes, riddles, songs, recipes, etc. on recipe cards to share with new friends and children along the way. If you have a special cake recipe and facilities are available, make one to share with new friends.

- When looking for local activities in a new city, check-out the daily newspaper, and the TV guide which can be understood in almost any language.

- While traveling long distances, mail home paper "extras" and items you've accumulated along the way but don't want to throw out: city maps, tourist pamphlets, attraction stubs, and receipts for tax purposes. Pack a pre-addressed manila envelope in your luggage and keep these items inside until you're ready to mail it home.

- If you're constantly traveling to the same destination, leave some duplicate toiletries there so you don't have to keep carrying them.

- Along the same idea, leave an old sweater, winter coat and winter shoes (or summer items) so you don't have to pack so much every trip.

My 31 Reasons to Travel with a Bandana

Almost every household has one... a Bandana. The funny thing is, many people haven't thought of traveling with one. Available in almost every color and design imaginable, they are one item that should be on every traveler's checklist. They take up almost no room and are particularly helpful in hot climates.

Here are some ideas on how to use a Bandana in your travels:

- Luggage Identification

- An emergency diaper

- Keep your head warm

- Ear warmer

- Protect bald or thinning heads from sun
- Protect the neck from the sun
- Scarf or head covering for places of worship
- Sweatband
- Wear damp around neck to stay cool
- Napkin
- Washcloth
- Travel Towel
- Rope
- First Aid- sling or bandage
- Knapsack
- Gift
- Bicycling (wrap around pant legs)
- Rag
- Face and nose covering for dust/sun/cold
- To sit on in the woods or park bench
- Sink stopper
- Wave as a distress signal flag
- Put under your feet on a train seat
- Table cloth for picnics, trains, buses
- Ribbon to tie your hair back
- Cover pillow on the plane

- Handle on a bag

- A filter for water or coffee

- Tie 3 together = Belt or a top

- Handkerchief (the original use)

- To wave goodbye

Always remember when packing your bags, to pack your respect for people of different cultures. You will usually find that people throughout the world are happy to have you as a visitor — as long as you are considerate of them and their way of life.

Anne McAlpin,
Travel Expert

- 16 -
Socially Conscience Travel

For those wishing to reduce their impact on the environment, Green Travel is a new travel method that's quickly gaining popularity. Centered around the preservation of the earth, Green travelers focus on the ideal of "lightening one's load," and "traveling lighter with less" – concepts near and dear to me and ones I wholeheartedly endorse!

Green Travelers:

- Walk, cycle and use public transportation whenever possible.

- Rent hybrid cars.

- Stay at "green" scored hotels.

- Book trips with green travel providers.

- Volunteer their time, giving back to the community they visit.

- Offset the carbon footprints with monetary donations to offset the amount of carbon their trip "costs" the atmosphere.

The "Eco-tourist" is an ecologically and socially conscious individual who focuses on volunteering, personal growth and learning new ways to live on the planet. Typically, eco-tourists visit destinations rich in flora, fauna and cultural heritage, hoping to enrich themselves by gaining a deep understanding of the environment and people they encounter.

Ecotourism programs aim to minimize the negative aspects of conventional tourism on the environment while working to enhance local cultural customs. At the forefront of the ecotourism movement, there is a keen awareness for the development and promotion of recycling, energy efficiency, water conservation and creation of economic opportunities.

Many tips throughout this book promote green & eco travel, but here are a few additional ones. The general idea is to reuse, renew & recycle!

- Ziploc® Bags can be reused for almost anything

- If you still have film canisters, these are great for small items like coins, jewelry, safety pins, etc.

- Use gel instead of antibacterial wipes – no litter! Then recycle the empty bottle.

- SIGG® Bottles – instead of throw-away bottles that may become toxic, use these safe, reusable ones over and over for any type of liquid.

- Recycle kids backpacks as travel bags – save money!

- Travel with the recycled "shopping bags" available at most stores, farmers markets & co-ops. Europe has been shopping this way for years – avoiding the waste of disposable bags. Save money by bringing your own to shop and save room, as they pack flat.

- Speaking of shopping – support the local economy

in the town you are in instead of the big stores you know! Think organic and locally-grown whenever possible – you'll find that your trip and taste buds will be rewarded!

- Rent a Hybrid or electric car whenever possible.

- Check out eco and enviro tours! Many companies offer these environmentally and earth friendly trips.

- Photos you develop on your journey can be used as postcards.

- Use re-chargeable batteries instead of disposable.

- Stay in hotels which offer less washing of sheets and towels. Choose to re-use your towel by hanging it on the rack, instead of leaving it on the floor.

- Consider your regular razor, rather than the disposable kind.

- Recycle and trade your old books, magazines and newspapers with others you meet – don't forget travel attendants!

- Donate old clothes – don't just discard them in your hotel room.

- Eco-travelers tend to pack/wear clothing made from more earth-friendly, sustainable fibers such as cotton, linen, hemp and bamboo.

- Check out Chapter 17 - Family Travel - in this book for great ideas for re-purposing kitchen supplies for children.

- When traveling by car, take some real utensils (and perhaps a picnic basket) that you can use instead of plastic take-out silverware.

- Plastic garbage bags are useful as luggage covers in the rain, for wet clothes, for a drop-cloth on a wet lawn and as a raincoat!

- Biodegradable soap is a must.

- 17 -
Family Travel Tips

There's no doubt that family travel makes memories... however what type of memories are made can depend on how prepared you are before you leave home.

Remember when planning family travel to take the age of each person into consideration. Each age has varying needs and varying needs means more to pack. More to pack translates into, "What bags am I going to take?" and "How's it all going to fit?" Here are some ideas on which bags are best and how to make the most of them. To make planning your trip easier, there's also a checklist of what to pack.

Duffel bags are the perfect solution for packing large items often needed by families, like strollers and car seats. Duffel bags with wheels are a welcome new luggage piece. Consider these rolling duffels, which can be lifesavers when your bag is really loaded. They also make it easier for the kids to help-out.

Small backpacks are great for children to carry-on the plane or use in the car. Help each child/teenager pack their bag and include things to keep them busy, like games, iPods®, CD's and snacks. Wrap-up some small gifts to give them along the way, things you'd normally buy for the trip but give the added element of surprise.

A wheeled carry-on tote bag, which fits under the seat of the plane, is great for mom, dad or mature traveler who'd rather not carry their bag and is easily accessible when items are needed in flight.

Plastic compression bags are the perfect solution to packing bulky items such as diapers, blankets and fleece jackets that can take up lots of room in your bag. Just squeeze out the air and you've saved up to 30% of valuable space. Great for stuffed animals, too.

Don't forget the space inside shoes — it's amazing how much will fit inside a teenager's shoe! Since travel-size bottles aren't enough for a week for most families, pack a full size bottle of shampoo, conditioner, etc. in a large Ziploc® bag and stick it in their shoes. You can stuff socks and underwear in there too!

By planning ahead, you'll save time and money and be able to enjoy valuable time with your family, instead of shopping for sunscreen when you'd rather be at the beach.

And remember this tip: Count your bags and family members as often as possible. You don't want to misplace either along the way!

Tips

A great idea for packing children's clothing is to put an entire days outfit (including underwear and socks) in a large freezer bag and write the child's name on the outside of the bag. This helps when traveling with more than one child and saves time searching through luggage for individual items.

• Don't forget the need to pack play clothes if traveling

on a more formal trip. Children will always find time to get dirty.

- A bandana is good for an emergency diaper!

- When traveling with children, get them involved. From the first moment you start planning your trip, up to and including the packing. Start with hanging a map on the wall (at their eye-level) and highlight the route you'll be taking.

- Purchase barely-used toys at garage sales to keep kids entertained without spending a lot of money.

- Wrap small surprise travel essentials that you'd give your children anyway and make them into gifts that you can hand out during a long travel day: disposable camera, coloring book, etc. Be sure not to wrap anything you're taking on a plane.

- Decide a week in advance which clothes your kids will take. After they're washed, put them aside so they're clean for the trip.

- Pack disposable diapers in an extra suitcase and then you'll have an additional bag to use for purchases on your way home!

- Pack a few extra tote bags to use for beach bags, picnics, etc. along the way.

- Assign a specific colored tote for each family member.

Coordinate colored tote bags for specific tasks, like "red" for dirty laundry and "green" for clean.

- Here's a fun project: Have your children help you make bag tags for each of the bags. Neon colored construction paper and bright pens and stickers will keep them busy for hours. Cover with clear contact paper to help protect them and punch a hole and thread a brightly colored shoelace to tie it on the bag/backpack. For safety, never put your child's name on the tag, just fun designs. They'll have a blast spotting their bag in a crowded baggage terminal.

- When traveling with your children, keep a recent photo of your children with you at all times, in case you become separated from them.

Beach Tips

- Pack an inflatable kids swimming pool for a trip to the beach. Tides can be dangerous for children and the water too cold. Fill it up and keep it away from the water (always with an adult in attendance). Kids can still make sand castles and stay cool with water from the pool. And the water gets warm quickly from the solar heat.

- Keep an inexpensive waterproof camera in your beach bag to catch some great shots in and out of the water. Keep your good camera away from the sand and salt water.

- Don't forget biodegradable travel soap to rinse out salt water from expensive swim suits. It also works as body wash and as shampoo.

- Flip-flops are your friends and are a must for scary public showers, hot sandy beaches, hot concrete parking lots, and scorching blacktop.

- To travel lighter, pack a double duty sunscreen and

insect repellent in one spray or wipes.

- Pack baby powder to avoid irritation caused from sand in swimsuits.

- Don't forget a lightweight, long sleeve shirt, pants or skirt to help protect against too much sun. Check **www.packitup.com** for UVA protection clothing.

Family Travel Checklist

Here is a list of items to consider taking, depending on the age of the travelers. Some are a must, others are optional. It depends on your destination. Keep this list with each family member's clothing list to help organize your next trip.

Travel Bags
- ❏ Wheeled duffel bag(s)
- ❏ Small backpack for each child
- ❏ Backpack for each adult
- ❏ Wheeled carry-on tote
- ❏ Extra collapsible tote bag(s)

Family Essentials
- ❏ Diapers and wipes
- ❏ Car Seats (check each state's requirements)
- ❏ Window sunscreen
- ❏ Sunscreen/hat
- ❏ Umbrella Stroller
- ❏ Convertible stroller/backpack
- ❏ Collapsible crib
- ❏ Blanket/pillow
- ❏ Pacifier

- ❏ Ear plugs
- ❏ Cell Phone/charger
- ❏ Garmin® or other GPS device
- ❏ 2 way radios (or multiple cell phones)
- ❏ First aid kit
- ❏ Medications
- ❏ Night Light
- ❏ Electrical outlet covers
- ❏ Antibacterial Hand Sanitizer
- ❏ Easy-care, easy-wear clothing

Food

- ❏ Water Bottles w/water not juice
- ❏ Healthy snacks (not greasy chips)
- ❏ Picnic supplies (plates, cutlery, etc.)
- ❏ Tippy cups, plastic bowls
- ❏ Pre-moistened towelettes

Children's Basic Weekend Travel Wardrobe

- ❏ 2-3 T-Shirts
- ❏ 1-2 pair Shorts
- ❏ 1-2 pair pants
- ❏ 3-4 underpants
- ❏ 2-3 Socks
- ❏ Sneakers
- ❏ Sandals
- ❏ Swimsuit and beach towel
- ❏ Sunglasses
- ❏ Pajamas
- ❏ Long-sleeved shirt

❏ Sweatshirt/sweatpants
❏ Rain jacket with hood
❏ Hat, gloves, boots
❏ Dress clothes/shoes/coat (if appropriate)

Toys

❏ CD player/headphones/batteries
❏ iPod®/Charger
❏ DVD Player/movies/charger
❏ Inflatable Beach ball
❏ Colored pencils (Crayons can melt)
❏ Bubbles (fun at any age)
❏ New toy

"A vacation is what you take when you can no longer take what you've been taking."

Earl Wilson

- 18 -
Travel Gift Ideas

Whether you are traveling to visit old friends, or making new friends along the way, it is always a nice gesture to bring a gift. It doesn't need to be expensive, and obviously, the easier it is to pack the better. It's the thought that counts.

Keep in-mind when selecting presents, that anything with a place name or logo on it is treasured by foreigners. In addition, something with a picture of your home state or region can be interesting to others and often leads to engaging conversation.

Instead of using valuable packing space in your luggage for wrapping paper and ribbons, pack a few small gift bags and tissue. Throw in a few gift cards and you're ready to celebrate any special occasion on the road.

Following are some gift ideas that are easy to pack and lightweight:

Balloons- For a fun game, hold a balloon behind your back and have children guess what color it is. The first one who guesses correctly wins the balloon. If you do this, for example, in Spanish, you teach them the color in English! It can be done anywhere in the world in any language.

Bubbles- Anywhere you go in the world, children love bubbles. They produce instant smiles! Pack inside lots of plastic bags.

Playing Cards- With fun pictures on them. National parks, flags, your company logo, cartoon characters, anything that's unique.

Specialty Foods- Small pre-packaged treats such as premium nuts, teas, salsas and candy make great gifts. Keep in-mind, chocolates melt.

Digital Camera- A fun way to immediately share some photos and entertain new friends along the way.

Polaroid Camera- Take a Polaroid camera for instant pictures.

Frisbee- A Frisbee packs easily and is a lot of fun. They are even more appreciated with a logo printed on them. This also may begin a game or two along the route and is great exercise, as well.

Picture Calendar- A calendar from your home region is a greatly appreciated and useful gift. It packs flat on the bottom of your suitcase and allows you to share the beauty of your region, which may be very different from the country you're visiting. They'll remember you every month.

Pins- Any type of pin is fun and can be worn on almost anything; hats, lapels, sweaters, anywhere. From your local regatta to your state flower.

Pens and Pencils- Popular gift idea. A variety of colors and sizes will be appreciated by all ages. They make good tips and gifts for people along the way, as some customs do not allow monetary gratuities.

Baseball Hats/Scarf- Lightweight and easy to pack, these are easy items to take. A hat with the logo of your favorite team or sport is great.

Stickers- From elections, sporting events or your own

home town, stickers are fun for children and adults.

Holiday Ornaments- For a memorable gift or souvenir, ornaments don't take up much space in your luggage. Every year, when you unpack your ornaments, it's like taking a trip around the world. From Nutcrackers discovered in Germany, to boomerangs from Australia, ornaments make unique and special gifts.

Bringing Gifts Home

Before you leave home, make a list of everyone you intend to gift upon your return. Start with the most important and continue down. Don't forget the pet sitter or the neighbor who takes care of your home while you are gone. A list will ensure that you don't over or under buy.

Plan in advance and pack bubble wrap if you're packing something breakable. If you're looking for a special poster or piece of art, poster tubes can be difficult to find when traveling. Pack one in your suitcase and use the inside of the tube to pack your socks and other squishible, non wrinkling clothing. Many stores will ship for you.

Don't forget all the great travel essentials mentioned throughout this book for wonderful, useful gifts for family and friends at home and along your travels. A hanging toiletry kit or luggage make wonderful graduation gifts or much appreciated wedding gifts.

"The journey, not the arrival matters."

T.S. Eliot

- 19 -
Travel Scarf Tying

A scarf is the most versatile accessory in your travel wardrobe. It can redefine any look and create styles that are casual or formal, professional or adventurous.

By including the following scarves in your travels and using this chapter as your guide, you will learn how to extend your wardrobe without using valuable luggage space. You will also add glamour to your wardrobe without spending a lot of money.

Three scarves that I like to travel with are: Oblong 10"x54", Square 34"x34" and a Sarong 46"x60".

Scarf Tips

- Pack scarves in plastic bags to keep wrinkles to a minimum.

- Silk scarves and natural fabrics are warmer than synthetics. Tuck them around the neck of your sweater to keep warm.

- Scarves make great gifts. They pack flat and don't break.

- The quality of scarves can vary greatly. Look for scarf edges that are rolled and stitched by hand, usually indicating a higher quality of scarf than those stitched by machine.

Orient Express

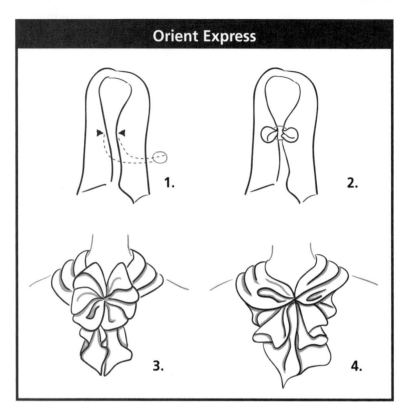

1. Drape oblong scarf around your neck.

2. Pinch only the inside edges of scarf at mid-way point.

3. Using a small covered elastic band, pull the edges slowly through until it forms a bow.

4. For another, more tailored look, place the elastic band in the back and pull the edges through towards you (the bow will be hidden).

As the name implies, this is a fast and elegant enhancement to any outfit, and works well with either silk or synthetic fabric. A small covered elastic band weighs less than a scarf-clip and usually works better (and less to pack!).

English Accent

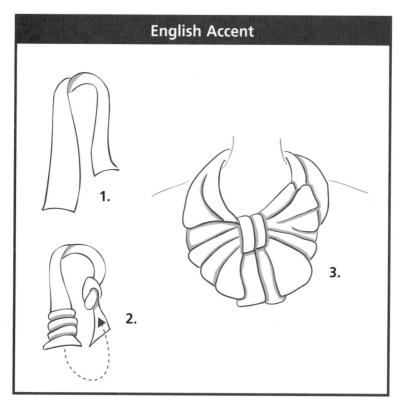

1. Place oblong scarf around neck keeping one end shorter than the other.

2. Tie a loose knot in the short end and fan pleat the long end until it's even with the short end. Hold pleats together and push up half-way through the knot.

3. Tighten the knot and fan as desired.

This works well with light synthetic fabrics. Worn with basic black or navy, it dresses up any outfit.

Segovian Secret

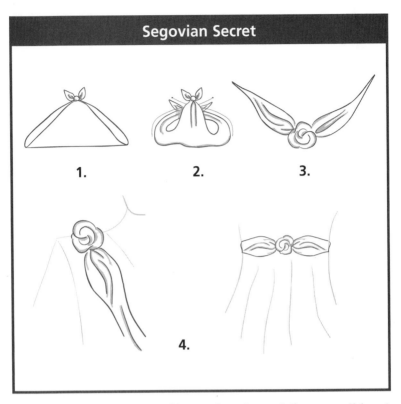

1.   2.   3.

4.

1. Fold square scarf into triangle and tie a small knot in top corner.

2. Take opposite ends and cross beneath the small knot, exchange hands.

3. Holding the ends, gently let the weight of the knot slowly slide down until the rose is formed.

4. Drape over shoulder for dramatic effect or around neck, waist or brim of a hat.

This works best with a silk scarf. Try a few different scarves to see varying results. Use a small safety pin to secure "rose" to garment.

English Accent

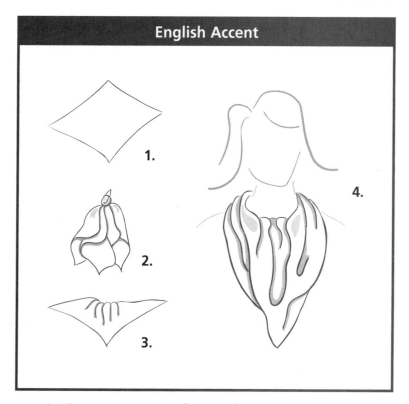

1. Place square scarf on a flat surface, wrong side up.

2. Tie a small knot at the center.

3. Fold scarf into a triangle with the knot on the inside.

4. Place the triangle in the front of the neck and tie at the back of the neck, arrange drape as desired.

This can be used as a substitute blouse under a V-neck sweater, cardigan or blazer. Perfect when traveling and laundry facilities are nowhere in sight!

Dutch Cap

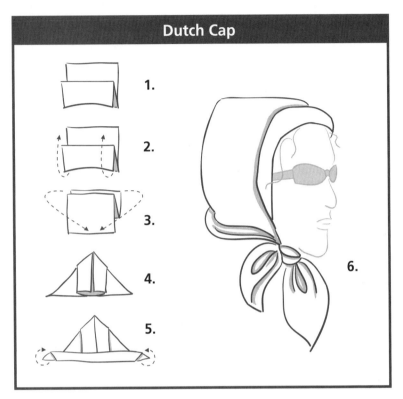

1.

2.

3.

4.

5.

6.

1. Place square scarf right side up on a flat surface. Fold the bottom edge to the top and then back down in half.

2. Taking bottom corners, turn scarf over, away from you.

3. Fold top two corners down to the center so they meet at the bottom edge.

4. Scarf will appear as shown.

5. From bottom, tightly roll the scarf until opening appears underneath.

6. Drape on head and tie under chin. Fold back edge framing face.

Works well with any type of fabrics. For warmth in very cold weather, use wool scarf instead of packing a wool hat. Saves space and your hairstyle.

St. Tropez Nights

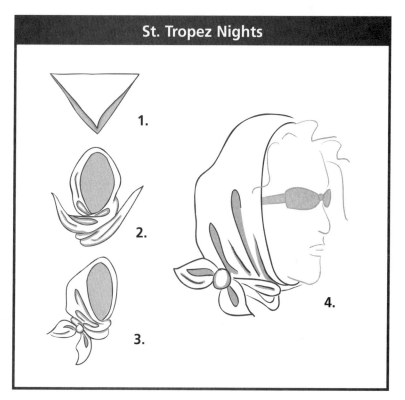

1. Fold a square scarf into a triangle.

2. Drape over head and cross the ends under chin.

3. Bring ends around to the back of neck and tie.

4. Arrange to frame face.

A touch of glamour, works well with any type of fabric. Good for a walk on a chilly evening or as a head covering for places of worship.

North Cape

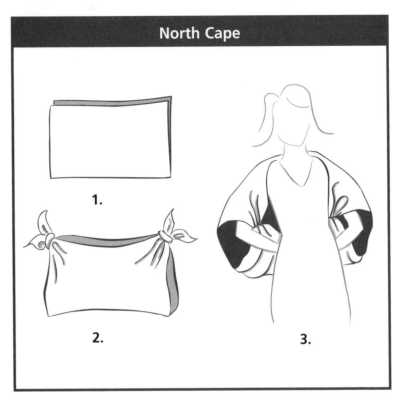

1.

2.   3.

1. Fold Sarong right sides together into a rectangle.

2. Tie the two corners together on each end.

3. Turn the Sarong right side out and place your arms through the openings, keeping the knots under your arms.

This is great for taking cover from the hot sun or keeping warm in air-conditioned restaurants. For a more formal look, use a fancier Sarong or make one by simply cutting any type of fabric and finishing the edges. (An interesting outing in a foreign country is to a fabric store. Thai silk works beautifully.)

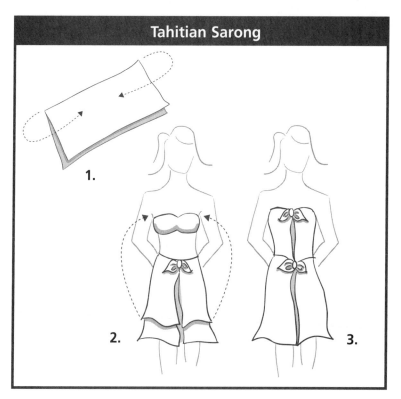

Tahitian Sarong

1. Fold Sarong in half with right sides together.

2. Place fold at waist and knot.

3. Take top layer from bottom edge and knot under your arm.

You can adjust the opening to the side for another look. Always travel with a sarong to use as a cover-up, beach towel or as a light blanket in a pinch.

"When in doubt, leave it out!"

Unknown

- 20 -
The Ultimate
Travelers Checklist

Here it is! A quick reference checklist to help get you organized before you pack your bags. This is a list of items to consider taking with you, depending on your destination. Some are a must, others optional. Keep this list with your own personal clothing list to help organize your next trip. Please refer to pages 145 for children's items. Also included are some essential tips to prepare you and your home for your trip.

Find some time a few weeks before your trip to go through the list, checking off items that you think you might need. This will give you time to gather/purchase items without last minute shopping. Feel free to make copies for ease of use—or print them from my website at **www.packitup.com**.

This checklist probably includes the entire contents of your house. Check off only items that you think will be essential for each destination. Cross-off the items you don't need and you'll be packing lighter. Be sure to make copies in order to have extras ready for your next trip!

The Ultimate Traveler's Checklist:

Home Checklist
- ❏ Stop Deliveries/ newspapers
- ❏ Have Post Office hold mail
- ❏ Arrange for care of pets, lawn and houseplants
- ❏ Set-up a timed night lighting system
- ❏ Notify local police of your absence
- ❏ Leave house key and trip itinerary with a neighbor, plus contact information and insurance numbers.
- ❏ Empty refrigerator
- ❏ Eliminate possible fire hazards (unplug appliances, etc.)
- ❏ Turn down thermostat
- ❏ Turn off water heater
- ❏ Store valuables in a safe place
- ❏ Lock all doors and windows
- ❏ Set automatic sprinklers

Pre-Departure
- ❏ Reconfirm with airlines
- ❏ Passport and Visas
- ❏ Health Documentation
- ❏ Transportation Tickets
- ❏ Student ID/Hostel Pass
- ❏ Emergency Information
- ❏ International Drivers License
- ❏ Insurance
- ❏ Hotel Reservations
- ❏ Small amount of local currency
- ❏ Credit Cards/ATM Card
- ❏ Trip Cancellation Insurance

❏ Medical Insurance
❏ Personal Identification
❏ Extra Passport Photos
❏ Only keys needed upon return home
❏ Photocopies of all documentation

Safety and Security
❏ Security Wallet
❏ Passport Cover
❏ ID/Boarding Pass Holder
❏ Travel flashlight
❏ Neon ID Tags
❏ Neon Luggage Tags and Straps
❏ Neon Cable Ties
❏ Adjustable-length Cable Lock
❏ Combination Locks
❏ Cell Phone and Charger/Adapter
❏ Rubber Door Stopper
❏ Travel Smoke Alarm
❏ Whistle/Compass Combo

Basics
❏ Luggage
❏ Convertible Day Bag
❏ Travel Wallet
❏ Small Day Pack
❏ Travel Clothing
❏ Rain Coat with Hood
❏ Gloves, Hat (visor or brimmed)
❏ Camera, Film, Memory Cards
❏ Camera Batteries or Charger

- ❏ Video Camera, Tapes
- ❏ Laptop Computer/Cables
- ❏ Compression Bags
- ❏ Packing Folders
- ❏ Packing Cubes
- ❏ Ziploc® Bags
- ❏ Expandable Tote
- ❏ Water Bottle
- ❏ Healthy Snack
- ❏ Language Books
- ❏ Travel Watch/Alarm
- ❏ Guidebooks/Maps
- ❏ Highlighter Pen/Marker
- ❏ Reading Material
- ❏ Note pad/Pens/Pencils
- ❏ Address Book/Labels
- ❏ Postcards/Family Photos
- ❏ Travel Alarm Clock
- ❏ Safety Pins
- ❏ Swimsuit
- ❏ Bandana/Scarf/Sarong
- ❏ Pocket Knife
- ❏ Anti-bacterial Hand Sanitizer/Wipes

Personal Care Items
- ❏ Hanging Toiletry Kit
- ❏ Comb/Brush
- ❏ Toothbrush/Paste
- ❏ Toothbrush Cap Covers
- ❏ Shampoo/Conditioner
- ❏ Sunscreen/Lip Balm

❑ Dental Floss
❑ Tissues/Toilet Paper
❑ Toilet Seat Covers
❑ Mouthwash
❑ Deodorant
❑ Feminine Hygiene Products
❑ Soap-Personal
❑ Skin Care Moisturizer
❑ Skin Care Cleanser and Toner
❑ Body Lotion/Body Powder
❑ Cotton Balls/Q-tips
❑ Shatterproof Mirror
❑ Make Up/Remover Pads
❑ Nail Polish/Remover Pads
❑ Nail File/Nail Clippers
❑ Tweezers
❑ Travel Perfume Atomizer
❑ Slippers/Socks
❑ Travel Bubble Bath
❑ Razor and Shaving Cream
❑ Travel Towel/Washcloth
❑ Shower Cap/Flip Flops
❑ Plastic Travel Bottles
❑ Dual Voltage Hair dryer
❑ Dual Voltage Curling Iron
❑ Extra Eye Glasses/Repair Kit
❑ Contacts/Contact Lens
❑ Contacts Cleaner/Solution

Medical
Always consult your personal physician or local health center for help in planning your travel related medication needs.

❏ Prescription Medication
❏ Insulated Bag for Medication (if needed)
❏ Bandaids
❏ First Aid Kit
❏ Aspirin/Pain Reliever
❏ Collapsible Cup
❏ Antihistamines
❏ Thermometer
❏ Cold Medicine
❏ Diarrhea Medicine
❏ Pepto-Bismol®/Alka-Seltzer®
❏ Laxative
❏ Insect Repellent
❏ Dental Repair Kit
❏ Sunscreen
❏ Lip Balm
❏ Sunburn Relief
❏ Antibiotic Cream
❏ Moleskin
❏ Motion Sickness/Jet Lag Remedy
❏ Personal Hygiene Items
❏ Water Purification System
❏ Vitamins

Comfort Items
❏ Neck Pillow, Eye Shades, Ear Plugs
❏ Travel Blanket

- Inflatable Lumbar Pillow
- Eye drops
- Removable Shoe Inserts
- iPod®/CD Player/CD's
- Book on Tape
- Photos From Home
- Travel Journal/Postcards
- Flask

Laundry on the Go
- Multi-Purpose Travel Soap
- Micro-fiber Travel Towel
- Braided Elastic Laundry Line
- Inflatable Hangers
- Sink Stopper
- Stain Stick Remover
- Sewing Kit
- Compression Bags for Laundry
- Dryer Sheets
- Travel Iron/Steamer
- Lint Brush

Additional Items
- Money Exchanger/ Calculator
- Coin Organizer
- Duct Tape/String
- Travel Umbrella
- Disposable Waterproof Camera
- Binoculars
- Dice
- Calculator

- ❏ Scissor
- ❏ Waterproof Neck Pouch
- ❏ Collapsible Cup
- ❏ Powdered Energy Drink
- ❏ Small Tape Recorder
- ❏ Stationary
- ❏ Expandable Tote Bag
- ❏ Extension Cord
- ❏ Sarong
- ❏ Flip Flops
- ❏ Evening Bag
- ❏ Travel Jewelry Case
- ❏ Travel Umbrella
- ❏ Corkscrew/Bottle Opener/ Straw
- ❏ Picnic Supplies
- ❏ Hot Pot
- ❏ Voltage Converters/ Adapters
- ❏ Collapsible Cane
- ❏ Book Light
- ❏ Rubber Bands/Paper Clips
- ❏ Business Cards
- ❏ Tape Measure
- ❏ Bubble Plastic (breakables)
- ❏ Extra Shoelaces
- ❏ Sunglasses/Sunscreen/Hat
- ❏ Walkie Talkies
- ❏ Backseat Organizer
- ❏ Sleepsack (silk/cotton)
- ❏ Short Wave Radio
- ❏ Insect Repellent
- ❏ Emergency Blanket

- ❏ Rain Poncho
- ❏ Mosquito Netting
- ❏ A Positive Attitude

Easy Gifts to Pack
- ❏ Calendar
- ❏ Playing Cards
- ❏ Bubbles
- ❏ Frisbee
- ❏ Bandana/Hat/Scarf
- ❏ Inflatable Beach Ball

"The journey, not the arrival matters."

T.S. Eliot

Resources

Transportation Security Administration
www.tsa.gov

Federal Aviation Administration
www.faa.gov

Travel Goods Association
www.travel-goods.org

American Society of Travel Agents
www.asta.org

CLIA- Cruise Lines International Assoc.
www.cruising.org

Medic Alert Foundation
(888) 633-4298
www.medicalert.com

World Health Organization
www.who.int

U.S. Department of State
www.state.gov

US State Department Travel Advisories and Consular Fact Sheets
http://travel.state.gov/travel_warnings.html

CIA World Fact Book
www.cia.gov/cia/publications/factbook/index.html

Zierer Visa Services
www.zvs.com

Travel Tip Contest

If in your travels you discover a new packing or travel tip that is not already included in **Pack It Up**, please enter it in our Travel Tip Contest at **www.packitup.com**.

All Travel Tip Winners will receive a **Pack It Up** Travel Essentials Gift Bag filled with items no traveler should leave home without!

Contact Anne

You can reach Anne directly at **anne@packitup.com**.

Happy Travels!

Pack It Up Seminars

To find out more about Anne's **Pack It Up**
Traveling Smart & Safe Seminars, please
go to **www.packitup.com**.

Notes & Quotes

"On a long journey, even a straw weighs heavy."

Spanish Proverb

Notes & Quotes

_____

_____

_____

_____

_____

_____

_____

_____

_____

"*When in Rome, do as the Romans do.*"

Anonymous

Notes & Quotes

_____

_____

_____

_____

_____

_____

_____

_____

_____

_____

"The only sure way of catching a train
is to miss the one before it."

G. K. Chesterton

Notes & Quotes

_____

_____

_____

_____

_____

_____

_____

_____

_____

*"He who would travel happily must
travel light."*

Antoine De Saint-Exupery

Start here, go anywhere.

Where are you going? What do you need? The AAA Travel Store can help! Whether you're traveling by plane, train, or automobile, the AAA Travel Stores have hundreds of travel-related products to keep you safe, comfortable, and organized.

Call or visit your local AAA Travel Store today.
We are open Monday through Friday, 8:30am to 5:30pm.

Your AAA Oregon/Idaho Travel Stores *

OREGON

Beaverton
503-243-6444

Bend
541-382-1303

Clackamas
503-241-6800

Coos Bay
541-269-7432

Corvallis
541-757-2535

Eugene
541-484-0661

Grants Pass
541-479-7829

Lake Oswego
503-973-6555

Medford
541-779-7170

Pendleton
541-276-2243

Portland
503-222-6720

Roseburg
541-673-7453

Salem
503-584-5200

Springfield / Gateway
541-741-8200

Warrenton
503-861-3118

IDAHO

Boise
208-342-9391

Meridian
208-884-4222

Pocatello
208-237-2225

Twin Falls
208-734-6441

* Visit our website for locations and directions

1-877-422-2359
www.AAA.com

Anne McAlpin's line of travel products and other unique accessories are available at discounted prices for AAA members.
Visit your nearest AAA Travel Store today.

Oregon/Idaho

1-877-422-2359
www.AAA.com